High Street
Monasteries

High Street Monasteries

Fresh expressions of committed Christianity

Ray Simpson

kevin mayhew

kevin
mayhew

First published in Great Britain in 2009 by Kevin Mayhew Ltd
Buxhall, Stowmarket, Suffolk IP14 3BW
Tel: +44 (0) 1449 737978 Fax: +44 (0) 1449 737834
E-mail: info@kevinmayhewltd.com

www.kevinmayhew.com

9 8 7 6 5 4 3 2 1 0
Hardback ISBN 978 1 84867 168 3
Catalogue No. 1501179

Cover design by Rob Mortonson
© Image Copyright: magicinfoto. Used under licence from Shutterstock Inc
Edited by Delian Bower and Alison Evans
Typeset by Chris Coe

Printed and bound in Great Britain

Contents

About the author

Ray Simpson is the founding guardian of the international Community of Aidan and Hilda and the principal tutor of its Celtic Christian Studies programme. He lives on the Holy Island of Lindisfarne where many pilgrims come to the Community's Retreat House library and Spirituality Centre, the Open Gate. An Anglican priest, he was previously also a Free Church minister in a new church plant sponsored by six church streams at Bowthorpe, Norwich. Ray is the author of numerous bestselling books on Celtic Spirituality. He writes a weekly blog on www.aidanandhilda.org.

Introduction

The 2005 BBC TV series *The Monastery*, which filmed five decidedly unmonastic members of the public as they shared their lives with the monks of Worth Abbey, UK, for 40 days, proved so popular that it was repeated that year in other lands, and was followed by *The Monastery Revisited* and a new series on *The Convent*. The ensuing book *Finding Sanctuary: Monastic Steps for Everyday Living* by Worth's Abbot Christopher Jamieson has had wide readership. In response to the many who now book retreats there, the Abbey has introduced its Compass programme: nine weekend retreats that introduce people to the monastic life. (see www.worthabbey.net)

Since about 1975 the Kirchentag, Germany's great annual gathering of Christian churches and movements, has had an 'Evangelical Monastery' area, where Christian communities are present to the many visitors. In Norway, a country that threw out monasteries, Oslo's biggest Pentecostal Church, Filadelfia, has established a community with three people who live together and pray the Hours together.

A Swedish Pentecostal pastor, Peter Haldof, has formed a community. Eight young people have taken vows for a year. They offer prayers four times each day, chant the psalms, wear robes, and live a rhythm of prayer and practical work. Peter Haldof believes that this is the future, that unless there is deep restitution, the church in Europe may not survive.[1]

Something new is in the air. A new tide comes in, as yet far out. Its name is the new monasticism. This book will explore this incoming tide.

[1] http://www.tidskriftenpilgrim.nu

Ivan Illich writes:

> Neither revolution nor reformation can ultimately change society – rather you must tell a new and powerful tale, one so persuasive that it sweeps away the old myths and becomes the preferred story – one so inclusive that it gathers all the bits of our past and present into a coherent whole, and shines light into the future so we can take one step forward.[2]

Could the new monasticism become this preferred story? Revolutions begin at the grassroots, not at the top of the pyramid of power. Those on that pyramid wait to be toppled, or just topple through old age. Those at the bottom wait to rise. Monasticism is a story of people at the bottom who have raised up their society, even when its leadership is toppled.

Our society groans under the weight of bureaucratic regulation. Jesus was 'at the bottom' but he raised up a new people. During his last, fateful week, when he was to complete all things, he chose his core of three most trusted friends to accompany him up to the mountain of transfiguration (Mark 9:2–13). There they witnessed, to their wonder, the two greatest representative figures in their history become manifest on each side of Jesus. Moses, the shaper of a people, gave a rule of life by which they were to live in their new situation. Elijah, the founder of the Order of Prophets, called out a creative minority to live by specific vows, in order that through them the whole of society might be renewed, as yeast transforms the dough.

Thus Jesus was strengthened by transformed elements of monasticism, though he transcended any one form of it. True monasticism is never an end – that would be to make it an idol – it is a means to a transformation, a fullness of humanness in Christ, and must only be followed in as much as it serves this purpose.

[2] Quoted in Costello, Tim, (1999) *Tips from a Travelling Soul-Searcher*, Allen & Unwin.

Old monasticism is perceived (wrongly, as a matter of fact) to be the standardised Orders of the Western Church, consisting of celibate monks and nuns with vows such as poverty, chastity and obedience which by their nature are not for ordinary, working people, and which, generally though not universally, are in sharp decline. The term new monasticism is being used to describe a broad range of emerging experiments, often by married as well as single people, which are not closed off from the stream of ordinary life, and which offer a challenging alternative to 'church'. New monasticism is sometimes perceived as a fresh expression of committed Christianity for the post-modern age. New monastics prefer to see it as pre-Christian rather than postmodern; it is a precursor of a third millennium which could be the most Christian age the world has yet experienced.

Last century the psychologist C. G. Jung prophesied that the collapse of western Christianity, and of society's ability to find transcendence, forced it to find escape routes from its prison of banality in fads, fashions, obsessions – even in war – that the profit-makers are happy to cater for. He thought that Christianity in its old form was now a wineskin beyond patching.[3] Jung thought that Christianity could only replenish the soul of modern man if it found a new symbolic imagery that could help humanity realise the greatness hidden in its soul.[4]

I believe that the life, death and resurrection of Christ is both a historical event and a primal symbolic pattern that has to be reconnected to the psyche of each generation through a reimagining and a reliving. Without this, our purely rational, surface philosophy will indeed, as Jung predicts, lead to disaster on an unparalleled scale. But with this, that tragedy

[3] Jung, C. G. (1963) *The Collected Works of C. G. Jung* (Vol 9) translated and edited by R. F. C. Hull, Routledge and Princeton University Press.

[4] This is well-expressed in Tacey, David, (2006) *How to Read Jung*, W. W. Norton & Co.

can be averted. In other words, could the new monasticism save the world?

I have included as an appendix a brilliant paper on biblical foundations for monastic living delivered by my colleague Simon Reed at the summer school on new monasticism at St John's College, Durham UK in 2007. Simon is vicar of the Church of the Ascension, Hanger Hill and St Mary's, West Twyford, in Ealing, West London. He studied theology to post-graduate level, specialising in New Testament studies, and is Deputy Guardian of the Community of Aidan and Hilda.

CHAPTER 1

The new monasticism

A first wave

The first wave of new monasticism came as a response to the Second World War, when civilisation seemed to be bleeding to death. Even before that war, in January 1935, Dietrich Bonhoeffer wrote in a prophetic letter to his brother Karl:

> The restoration of the Church must surely come from a new kind of monasticism, which will have only one thing in common with the old, a life lived without compromise according to the Sermon on the Mount in the following of Jesus. I believe the time has come to gather people together for this.[5]

Bonhoeffer fled to England. He visited Anglican monasteries and was impressed with some of their disciplines, such as the chanting of psalms at the Community of the Resurrection at Mirfield and at the Society of the Sacred Mission at Kelham. The 'Confessing' Church[6] asked him to lead an underground community at Finkenwald which trained ordinands. There Bonhoeffer wrote three seminal books, including *Life Together* and *The Cost of Discipleship*. In his preface to *The Cost of Discipleship*, John de Grochu highlights the plight of our contemporary church:

---

[5] Taken from a letter to his brother Karl-Friedrich Bonhoeffer from London on 14 January 1935, published in *A Testament in Freedom: The Essential Writings of Dietrich Bonhoeffer*, HarperSanFrancisco (1995) p. 424.

[6] The 'Confessing Church' was a group of German Evangelical Christians most actively opposed to the German Christian Movement within the Church sponsored by the Nazis. See http://www.encyclopedia.com/doc/1095-ConfessingChurch.html

> We have gathered like eagles around the carcass of
> cheap grace, and there we have drunk of the poison
> which has killed the life of following Christ.

Because of his execution in a prison cell shortly before the end of
the Second World War we shall never know how Bonhoeffer
would have developed a new monasticism. He does leave us
with certain clues. For example, he warned new communities
that two years is the danger time when dreams are dashed
against the rocks of reality, and disillusionment sets in:

> Only that fellowship which faces such disillusionment,
> with all its ugly and unhappy aspects, begins to be
> what it should be in God's sight ... Every human wish
> dream that is injected into the Christian community
> is a hindrance to genuine community and must be
> banished if genuine community is to survive. The one
> who loves their dream of community more than the
> community itself becomes a destroyer of the latter,
> even though their personal intentions may be ever
> so honest and sacrificial.

Sadly, the German Church did not take hold of what Bonhoeffer
had conceived. In Scotland, however, George MacLeod had
been developing the Iona Community during those same war
years. Bonhoeffer's *Life Together* became standard reading
there.[7]

The Iona Community

George MacLeod had been the Church of Scotland minister of
Govan Old Parish, Glasgow, during the hungry years of the
Great Depression, when many people were unemployed.
He resigned his charge because he felt the Church was not

[7] Bonhoeffer, D., (1954) *Life Together*, SCM.

meeting the needs of such people. Only by experiments, such as bringing together industrial workers and ministers, could faith thrive again in an industrial age. In 1899 the Duke of Argyle had given Iona Abbey and its grounds to a Trust on condition that the Abbey church be restored as an ecumenical place of worship. By 1938 the Abbey church had been restored but the living quarters were still in ruins. MacLeod negotiated that unemployed workers and novice ministers would rebuild these quarters together, and the new Iona Community would service them.

This dispersed community grew, and currently has several hundred members, up to two thousand Associate members and over three thousand Friends in a number of countries. Members follow a Rule, but do not take life vows; they renew their vows year by year and are free to leave at any time. The Rule's five parts are:

1. Regular prayer and Bible study

2. Sharing and accounting to their local group for the use of money – they are encouraged to give away 10 per cent of their disposable income

3. Sharing and accounting for their use of time

4. Meeting with the local group

5. Working for justice and peace, which requires opposition to weapons of mass destruction and support of the United Nations. In recent years 'justice' has embraced much of the liberal agenda, such as equality for gay people.

One of the community's most significant experiments, now sadly in the past, was the creation of 'Columba Houses'. These were allocated by a local council for one or more Iona community volunteers to act as a key worker in a deprived area.

The community communicates through its website and its magazine, *The Coracle*, and has spawned the Wild Goose Resources Group, which produces a rich vein of worship, devotional and biographical material. Currently it maintains three centres: the Abbey House and the MacLeod Centre on Iona, and Camas Adventure Camp on the Ross of Mull. Its administrative headquarters are in Community House, Govan, Glasgow, where some of the 25 staff engage in the needs of the city. They support ecumenical experiments such as *Holy City*, an event in Renfrew Street St Stephen's Church, where people can question and worship in their own style.[8] Members are required to elect a new leader every five years. The community believes this guards against paternalism, though it perhaps evades issues of divine calling and continuity.

Ian Bradley[9] sees the attractiveness of this community as its rootedness in the incarnation, its peace and justice work and its grittiness, born in the slums of Glasgow. It has its tensions. Ronald Ferguson relates, in his biography of the founder, how MacLeod himself, in his old age, felt the community had lost the Evangelical and Pentecostal dimensions that he himself had coveted.[10]

In recent years the community has held agonised debates as to whether the centres on Iona are distractions from its primary calling. On the one hand, many people who come for a six-day experience of community at the Abbey find something unique. On the other hand, many pilgrims are bemused that the work and the worship are often led by staff who are not living the community's Rule. There is no long-term community there that lives a Rule of prayer and work.

[8] See Ferguson, Ronald (1988) *Chasing the Wild Goose: The Iona Community*, Collins.

[9] The Revd Dr Ian Bradley is Reader in Practical Theology, St Mary's College at the School of Divinity, University of St Andrews.

[10] Ferguson, Ronald (1990) *George MacLeod: Founder of the Iona Community*, Collins.

Taizé

Taizé, the ecumenical community in France, is exactly the opposite. It began in 1940 when, at the age of 25, Roger Schulz left his native Switzerland to live in the small Burgundian village of Taizé. During long years of convalescence recovering from tuberculosis in Switzerland, a vocation to create a community had matured within him. Thanks to a modest loan, he bought at Taizé a house with outlying buildings, but no running water, where he and his sister offered hospitality to Jewish refugees. He was found out, and fled to Geneva where he drew a band of brothers who lived a common life. They returned to Taizé in 1944 and on Easter Day 1949, seven of them committed themselves to a life together in celibacy and great simplicity. In the silence of a long retreat, during the winter of 1952–53, Brother Roger wrote the Rule of Taizé, expressing for his brothers 'the essential that makes the common life possible'. This Rule includes: three times daily common prayer and common meals, values born of the Beatitudes, being open to all that is human, maintaining inner silence at all times, receiving guests as if they are Christ, pooling of goods, attentiveness to the abbot, who appoints his successor but roots out all authoritarianism in himself.[11]

One of the qualities of the brothers was deep listening to whoever God brought to them. An unexpected development in the 1960s was requests from young adults to camp nearby and join in the common prayer. As Brother Roger listened to them, and tried to respond to their questions and concerns, and the number of such visitors grew hugely, the very shape of Taizé's hospitality and outreach was changed in order to meet their spiritual thirst. In 1974, to coincide with the opening of the Council of Youth, which brought 40,000 young people to

---

[11] See Brother Roger (1980) *Parable of Community: the Rule and Basic Texts of Taizé*, Mowbray and www.taize.fr.

Taizé, Brother Roger issued the first of a series of letters. At least two of these were written in Africa and South America, during visits in which Brother Roger and small groups of young people shared the lives and conditions of some of the world's poorest people.

Taizé has made a unique contribution to ecumenism. Its first brothers were all Protestant; now they also number Catholics. After Brother Roger received communion from then Cardinal Joseph Ratzinger at Pope John Paul II's funeral there were claims that he had secretly converted to the Roman Catholic faith. Brother Alois, the present prior, sought to clarify this in an interview with the French Catholic newspaper, *La Croix*.

> He explained that Brother Roger's path was 'progressive and totally new' and therefore 'difficult to explain and understand'. To speak of 'conversion' in this regard is to fail to understand the originality of what Brother Roger was looking for. The word 'conversion' is full of history, it implies a break with one's origins. Brother Roger accepted that for some people an individual conversion could be the way but for him and for our community, he preferred to speak of 'communion'. He continued, 'For Brother Roger, entering full communion with the Catholic Church centred on two points that he never kept secret, namely receiving the Eucharist and the need for a ministry of unity exercised by the Bishop of Rome.' It was in this sense that Brother Roger was able to say 'I have found my own Christian identity, reconciling in myself the faith of my origins with the mystery of the Catholic faith, without any rupture whatsoever.'

Although the community sponsors large youth meetings each year in a different city, it has refused to set up a Taizé movement, or Taizé churches, preferring to let the Holy Spirit inspire individuals and churches through its witness without the need for bureaucratic organisation. Brother Roger was once offered a hotel near Taizé. He refused it, because 'it would make things too complicated'!

Despite this, Taizé has spawned a unique style of worship music that reflects the meditative nature of the Community and is widely used throughout the world. Taizé music emphasises simple phrases, usually lines from psalms or other pieces of Scripture, repeated and sometimes also sung in canon. The repetition is intended to aid meditation and prayer.

The community is made up of over 100 brothers, Catholics and others from various Protestant backgrounds, from more than 25 nations. The brothers live by their own work. They do not accept gifts or donations for themselves. Some live in small groups – 'fraternities' – among the very poor. This one community has a worldwide outreach through 'pilgrimages of trust', in which brothers make visits and lead meetings, large and small, across the globe.

Focolare

The Focolare movement was born among Catholics in Italy in the early 1940s as war raged. Focolare means 'hearth', and the movement's supreme virtue is unity. This lay movement became ecumenical, spread to 180 countries and has 140,000 members. Many of its innovations, such as a return to Scripture and a reassessment of the importance of the laity, anticipated the direction the Second Vatican Council would take. Its members, married or single, commit to unity with Jesus in gatherings round the Word of God, and with each other. Its spirit, aims and infrastructure are defined in a statute which was approved by the Holy See in 1990. The international coordinating centre of the movement is at Rocca di Papa, near Rome. This movement has many expressions, including

The Economy of Communion, the Gen, for young people, the Volunteers, the New Families Movement, 20 little model towns, and the annual mariapolis. The new monastic element consists of the Focolarini. They live as groups of either men or women in the Focolare houses and work in the world outside. They have left behind their families and countries; they try to keep the presence of Jesus among them by mutual love in all they do. They see the evangelical counsels of poverty, chastity and obedience as supports to maintain this unity by being detached from possessions, from other people and from oneself. They include married people who belong in a complete way, and not as second-class members.

The founder, Chiara Lubich, who died in 2008, gained Pope John Paul II's assent to the leader always being a lay person: she feared what clericalisation might mean. Some would say that the single-minded pursuit of unity at almost any price undercuts the prophetic, evangelistic and charismatic spirit, and that unity was one way: recruits are urged to support the centre, and there is less evidence of the centre becoming one with those on the edges. Nevertheless, the Focolarini houses are precious gifts to the world.[12]

Madonna House

The Madonna House apostolate has houses in several countries under the authority of the local Roman Catholic bishop. Members model themselves on charity and love as it was thought to have been lived in the holy family's house at Nazareth. It was founded in 1947 by the Russian Catherine Doherty and her husband Eddie. Today the community has more than 200 lay men, women and priests, dedicated to loving and serving Christ through promises of poverty, chastity, and obedience. Their spirituality is enshrined in 'The Little

[12] See *Chiara Lubich: A Life for Unity* (an interview by Franca Zambonini), New City (1992).

Mandate', which comprises words that Catherine believed she received from Jesus Christ such as:

> Sell all. Give it directly, personally to the poor. Little – be always little! Be simple, poor, childlike. Preach the Gospel with your life – without compromise! Listen to the Spirit. He will lead you. Do little things exceedingly well for love of Me. Go into the marketplace and stay with Me. Pray always, fast. Be hidden. Be a light to your neighbour's feet. Go without fear into the depth of men's hearts. I shall be with you.

Bose

Halfway between Milan and Turin, in a little hollow below a glacial moraine, with the foothills of the Italian Alps providing the distant horizon, sits the monastery of Bose, one of the most important religious foundations in Italy since the Second Vatican Council. On the day the Council closed, 8 December 1965, Enzo Bianchi, a 21-year-old layman, began to live a monastic life in an abandoned farm house. Three years later in August 1968 three others decided to join him at Bose. One of them was a pastor in the Swiss Reformed Church, and one was a woman. With them two of the chief characteristics of the monastic community of Bose were established: it would be ecumenical in membership and would include both men and women. The experiment had to survive the opposition of the local bishop, but thanks to the support of the cardinal archbishop of Turin, the community survived and grew and eventually won the formal approval of a later bishop.

The community now consists of some 80 members, with the men as a slight majority; the average age is around 40. Most of the members are from northern Italy, but several other European countries are represented, and there is one American. One member is the retired Orthodox Metropolitan of Sylivira, Emilianos Timiadis, who had served as personal representative of the Ecumenical Patriarch at the World Council of Churches. There are at least four Protestants in the community. The primary vocation is monastic and so only five of the monks are ordained priests to see to the sacramental needs of the community and of the thousands of guests who descend upon the monastery throughout the year. The community has its own monastic rule, which borrows from earlier monastic traditions but follows none of them exactly.

The day is structured around the common prayer. The monks arise at 4.30am for private prayer and then join in common morning prayer at 6am. The rest of the morning is devoted to the various activities that monks perform (from iconography to tending the gardens, from carpentry to writing, from translating to bottling teas, condiments, olive oil, and spices). Midday prayer is at 12.30pm, and after an afternoon of work and study, evening prayer is chanted at 6.30pm. The altum silentio runs from 8pm to 8am.The altum silentio means 'nourishing' and is similar to the term greater silence which others use.

The common prayer is sung in Italian with an adaptation of Gregorian chant sung in lovely harmonies. The texts of the Psaltery have been newly translated from the Hebrew and with an eye also to the traditional christological interpretation of the psalms. The spirituality cultivated at Bose is wholly centred upon the Word of God in the Scriptures, illumined also by the meditations of the Fathers and of the great spiritual masters.

The community has its own publishing house, Qiqayon (the Hebrew name of the shrub that grew up to shelter Jonah from the heat), which has published many texts of theology and of the various schools of Christian and Jewish spirituality. Monks offer regular courses in biblical Hebrew and Greek. Enzo Bianchi offers frequent 'Encounters' – talks on spiritual and theological themes.

Bianchi, prior of the community but never ordained himself, has become an important figure in the Church in Italy.

To accommodate the growing number of people who want to come to share the experience of prayer and spiritual commitment, the community recently opened a new guesthouse, and the monks are now constructing a better facility for those who wish to camp out at the monastery. Guests are welcomed regardless of their ability to pay, although recommendations for daily expenses are provided for those who can pay. Priests are available for confession, and monks for spiritual conversation. At least one respected church leader believes that Bose will succeed Taizé as the most influential community in Europe.

These are just a few of many such movements that were born in the years of post-war hardship, when clear-thinking people saw the need to model ways for society that would make a return to war unthinkable.

A second wave

A second wave of new monasticism came with the swinging sixties and seventies, with their moral permissiveness and material prosperity which left a vacuum and spawned a longing for community.

There was a proliferation of household communities inspired by the charismatic renewal. The Post Green Community in Britain and the Anne Arbor Community in the USA were notable. However, the sheer stress caused by people of contrary temperaments and conditioning living on top of each other, without the long processes of purifying, discernment and delegation associated with the monastic disciplines, meant that few of these proved to be sustainable. Strangely, however, several of these in secular France have survived.

Chemin Neuf

Chemin Neuf which was founded in 1973 comprises married

couples, families, consecrated women and men and priests (Catholic, Protestant, Orthodox) who have decided to bear witness together to their faith in Jesus Christ, and to work for Christian unity, though within a framework that comes under the authority of the Roman Catholic Church. It draws from the teachings of St Ignatius Loyola and St Teresa of Avila. Members live in neighbourhood fraternities (that is, they live separately but in the same neighbourhood) and in life fraternities (they live under the same roof). Most of them work in their professions or occupations, while others place themselves full-time at the service of the Church. The community's work pays for its daily life. After three years of discernment, the members opt either for a renewable three-year commitment or for a permanent commitment within the community, which can only be done after renewing the three-year commitment twice more. Chemin Neuf has about 1000 members in 20 countries.

The Community of the Beatitudes

The Catholic Community of the Beatitudes, founded in France in 1973 by Ephraim, his wife Jo, and another couple Jean-Marc and Mireille, is one of the communities expressing new forms of 'consecrated' life.

The community is – according to Canon Law – a Private Association of the Faithful, established in the archdiocese of Albi (France) in 1985. The community gathers in a spirit of chastity people of all states of life: married couples, brothers and sisters, celibates, deacons and priests. Each submits their time commitments to the Shepherd of their House and undertakes their outside work in the name of the community. Members strive to live the Beatitudes in a spirit of contemplative prayer and solicitude for the poor, within the framework of parishes, youth, families or media. The community has 1500 members and 86 houses in the five continents.

The Monastic Community of Jerusalem

The mission of the Monastic Community of Jerusalem, founded in Saint Gervais Church in Paris in 1975 by Fr Pierre-Marie Delfieux, is to live in the heart of the city, in the heart of God. The essence of their vocation is summed up in Jesus' prayer 'Father, I do not ask that you take them out of the world, but that you keep them from the evil one' (John 17:15). Their understanding is that since human beings are created as the most beautiful likeness of God, the monks and nuns and the lay associates of this community want to meet God in the inhabitants of the city. They work part-time in the city and carry it in their prayer. They want to create an oasis of silence and prayer in the desert of the city which is also a place of welcome and sharing. They rent their housing in order to avoid becoming too separate or settled. Having embraced the city's rhythms, they also keep the rhythm of morning, noon and evening prayer.[13]

Consecrated Virgins

A more ancient tradition was also revived at this time. In 1970 the Roman Catholic Church brought back the Rite for Consecrated Virgins who are not nuns, and who make their vow of mystical betrothal to Christ before their bishop.[14] In the Blue Mountains of Australia I met Fr Eugene Stockton, a lay hermit according to the Roman Catholic Code of Canon Law, Canon 603.

Anglicans have since followed suit. A book that is considered a must-read for anyone seriously considering vowed life is *Selling All* by Sandra M. Schneiders IHM,[15] which explores vocational discernment, formation, commitment and questions as to whether this is a valid form of religious life.

[13] See *A City Not Forsaken: Jerusalem Community Rule of Life*, DLT (2004).
[14] See 'Consecrated Virgins for Today's Church' in *Consecrated Life*, Vol. 24, No. 2 Chicago Institute on Religious Life (2002).
[15] Schneiders, Sandra M., IHM (2001) *Selling All*, Paulist Press.

Other monastic communities

There were other, little heard of, attempts at new monasticism during these decades. New Zealander Viv Grigg moved into a squatter settlement in Manila, Philippines, in the 1970s and lived a radical form of incarnational mission. In the 1980s and 1990s he published books calling the church to make room for Protestant missionary orders among the urban poor. Vows would play a key role, he explained, if these movements were to be effective: 'Workers will make covenants to live lifestyles of non-destitute poverty and simplicity for the sake of identification with the poor.' He even espoused the value of celibacy, at least for a period: 'The Protestant ethic, in its reaction to errant Catholicism, coupled with the breakdown of American family structures, has moved to an extreme worship of comfortable marriage that ignores the pressing urgency of the times and sacrifices needed to redeem the poor of the earth.'[16]

The movement for new communities on the whole bypassed conservative evangelical Christians. However, a generation after Bonhoeffer, the respected evangelical leader John Stott called for 'the re-monking of the church'. I asked him for the source of this, but in his veteran years he could not remember. John Stott has, against the tide, lived a life of consistent discipline, and I wonder whether his call for a 're-monking' is in fact a call to recover godly disciplines.

[16] Servant Movement: Protestant Missionary Orders with Vows of Non-Destitute Poverty (2000).See www.urbanleaders.org/Viv_Grigg/WHY3DORD.htm

A third wave

The Community of Aidan and Hilda

In the 1990s dispersed communities such as the Northumbria Community and my own Community of Aidan and Hilda came to birth. Their distinctive contribution is to combine the depth of the ancient monastic disciplines with the flexibility of today's global highway. The Community of Aidan and Hilda invites each person to journey with a soul friend and apply the common way of life in a way that enables their unique vocation to unfold and their humanity to come to full flower. It describes itself as an international body of Christians who journey with God, reconnecting us with the Spirit and the scriptures, the saints and the streets, the seasons and the soil. It seeks to cradle a Christian spirituality for today which renews the church and brings healing to fragmented people, communities and lands. It welcomes people of all backgrounds and countries who wish to be wholly available to God the Holy Trinity and to the way of Jesus as revealed to us in the Bible. The community offers a contemporary way of life that draws inspiration from many sources, including desert and Celtic Christians. It espouses a rhythm of prayer and study, simple lifestyle creation, care, mission and justice, seeking to weave together the separated strands of Christianity. Each member shares their journey with a Soul Friend. It has members on four continents and a sister community in the USA. Its aim is that indigenous communities of love spring up and it is in an early stage of developing link houses, projects and churches.

Community is fostered through the internet and magazine, visits, regional meetings and communal retreats. It has been led to earth its worldwide work on England's Holy Island of Lindisfarne. There a handful of members live the daily rhythm of prayer, work, hospitality and study focused around its retreat house (The Open Gate), office, resources and study centre.

It seeks to restore holistic learning, which some believe was lost when the universities were removed from the monasteries. Its courses offer 'honour, not honours.' The community's aim in writing such resources as the four-volume *The Celtic Prayer Book* (Kevin Mayhew 2003), is to contribute to a renewal of the Church's, as well as its own, worship. After some ten years the community set out its organisational framework and procedures for decision-making in its handbook. It is hard for me to be objective about my own community, but I sense that it was born for the internet age.

The community has thought through infrastructures for possible future developments. It remains to be seen whether or not any of these will take off. They include a basis for link cells, houses, churches, and sketes. A skete would consist of Voyagers in a locality who live according to an agreed common framework. A skete (a loose community) usually has a common area of worship with individual buildings. Voyagers are members of the community who have taken first vows. The locality typically would include four daily corporate spaces for prayer, at least a weekly meal, a weekly time for teaching and sharing, some common work or mission, a yearly retreat, and special events which all observe. The skete would set out ways of applying the Way of Life in decision-making, ethos, work and relationships. The skete members would each give account for their lives and finances to the community Guardian who would visit at least once a year. The skete members would nominate (by secret election) a long Voyager to be leader once every five years for approval by the Community's Guardian and its Soul Friend. Each skete member would be free to live their own life within this framework, and to be single or married. If the member was part of a family, the family needs to agree to respect the common framework. Each member would be responsible for their own dwelling, work and income. Members might agree to give surplus income to the skete. If a skete owns or rents common land it should have a zone of silence, ideally where the chapel is situated.

The Northumbria Community

The Northumbria Community was a fusion in 1994 of the Nether Springs Trust, founded by John Skinner and Andy Raine in the 1980s, which hosted spirituality workshops, and Northumbria Ministries, which was committed to evangelism in the north-east of England, and founded by Roy Searle in 1989. As the founders dialogued, a loose community formed around them. They drew up a Rule of Life, based on daily prayer, whose twin peaks were vulnerability and availability. They focused their programmes on the themes of cell and coracle, monastery and mission, desert fathers and Celtic saints. They leased a property in Northumberland, Hetton Hall, where a few members live and others come to stay, work, pray or study. They published a book of daily readings and liturgies entitled *Celtic Daily Prayer*[17] which has sold widely. Recusants from churches and artistic people in particular have found the community to be a spiritual home, and many are grateful for its attempts to rehabilitate dance and storytelling in the Christian scene.

Leadership has always been a live issue. The original Nether Springs leaders were asked to lay down their office. At the first transition of the founders to the few, the attempt to make a working Council, with members having areas of responsibility, was unable to deliver and Council became more like a sounding board for the leaders. This council was disbanded in 2004 and a General Chapter formed. This experienced uncertainty about its own style and whether or not it should function in business mode. It seems there are no procedures for how to replace a leader who dies, retires or becomes incapacitated.

[17] *Celtic Daily Prayer: Prayers and Readings from the Northumbria Community*, HarperOne (2002).

Urban Vision

In 1996 Urban Vision was formed in New Zealand/Aotearoa as a response to growing injustice. A group who had worked with Youth for Christ covenanted to build God's kingdom on the margins using three threads: the inward journey, the communal journey, and the external focus all of which come from the heart of God. At first they were almost anarchist, but experience has taught them what is necessary for sustainability. Now, they only choose issues to protest about which spring from the people they are in solidarity with. They have 42 adults and 21 children who make up six local communities sited in marginalised neighbourhoods. A significant minority are Maori Christians, the rest are Pakeha (white) Christians who engage with Maori perspectives and customs and work towards reconciliation. They are currently developing an indigenous sacred calendar that dovetails with the Anglican Church's existing one. All the children are developing a bicultural identity.

Urban Vision has an annual Hui (full gathering) on a nearby Marae (the ancestral home and gathering point of an Iwi or clan). On the Marae a Christian Kaumatua (wise elder) has embraced them and encouraged their faltering journey. They use Maori language to a greater or lesser extent. They learn much from their Maori brethren about the importance of holistic spirituality that incorporates a deep sense of community and responsibility for the planet, similar to Celtic spirituality.

Urban Vision have pioneered the Newtown film club with mental health consumers, community film competitions, development amongst many communities both indigenous and refugee/migrant, the Ngatiawa rural retreat centre, and successful community musicals. They are exploring whether to become an Order. Martin Robinson (author of books on the emerging Church and director of Together in Mission) writes:

The fun-loving, low-commitment, entertainment-driven prevailing church culture is quite at odds with where we are currently. We are more than a para-church because of our emphasis on community and development of spiritual rhythms ... do we stay non-denominational or choose a denomination? While some of us believe denominations are dying, many of us are sensing the need to be formally connected with a denomination, but which one?[18]

The Community of Friends in Renewal

An example of a monastic household is the Community of Friends in Renewal, also known as the Lindisfarne Community, led by Andrew and Jane Fitz-Gibbon at Ithaca, New York State. At the time of writing there are about 25 members, including children at Ithaca, and two small linked communities. About 15 attend weekly theology school. On Sundays there is an extended Eucharist. Although they came from a charismatic and free-spirited background, their study of monasticism led them to two conclusions. First, small communities need spiritual parents. Second, small communities have to be deeply connected to the whole church. Monasticism is grounded in a deep humility that has no false or grandiose illusions. It has a deep connectedness which also derives from a high theology that there is only one Holy, Catholic, Orthodox, Apostolic Church. These two convictions led the Fitz-Gibbons to become Abbott and Abbess (a husband and wife leadership team) and to be ordained by a bishop within the apostolic succession. In 2001 their community and ministries were chartered as a jurisdiction under the archbishop of the Communion of Evangelical Episcopal Churches. Their Rule is fairly loose – a statement of values such as charity, equality, fidelity, generosity,

[18] In Lyons Lee, Brent and Simpson, Ray (2008) *Emerging Down Under*, ATF Press.

hospitality, humility and integrity. In this understanding, a household fellowship becomes monastic when its members adopt a Rule and when its leadership is accountable to the wider church in a way that is recognised by the Church.[19]

The Missionary Order of St Thomas

The Missionary Order of St Thomas (TOM) is a dispersed community of multi-context missional leaders. It was inaugurated in Sheffield, UK, on 6 April 2003. It grew out of the Anglican-Baptist Ecumenical Project in the Crookes area of Sheffield, UK, whose missionary outreach and charismatic leadership, especially to young adults, based on the small group, cluster or large celebration model far transcended parish boundaries. Its members commit to the vows of simplicity, purity and accountability, and to 'life-shapes' – their rule or pattern of life. These consist of: the circle (learning from life); the semi-circle (rhythm); the triangle (focus); the square (stages of life); the pentagon (gifts and roles); the hexagon (connections); the heptagon (signs) and the octagon (people for life-sharing faith). These are really concepts, or aspirations, and it is hard to see how their practical outworking can be measured, although TOM says it is inspired by the monastic movements of previous eras. There are various TOM communities spread throughout the UK with larger hubs in Sheffield and Bristol. There are members in European countries, Australasia and the USA.

Currently the Senior Guardian is Mike Breen, the former Rector at St Thomas who is now on the staff at Community Church of Joy in Glendale, Arizona, and at Fuller Seminary in California. The Senior Guardian is elected for a period of six years by the full members meeting in chapter, and is accountable to them and to a visitor from the wider Church. It is hard to

---

[19] See http://www.icmi.org/ on the Lindisfarne Community.

see how someone in two such intense roles can fulfil an ade-quate pastoral or guidance role for dispersed members. Its strength is that it enables some of God's entrepeneurs to band together. Its weakness may be its lack of procedures for when things go wrong.

A fourth wave

The Simple Way Community

A fourth wave began in the mid-1990s among young people in the USA. A group of recent students at the Christian liberal arts school, near Philadelphia, read a newspaper article about some homeless families who had been evicted from a disused Roman Catholic cathedral. They befriended them, and eventually moved into the neighbourhood as The Community, sharing a large house together. Their only programme was 'to love God, love people and follow Jesus'. A former fellow student, Jonathan Wilson-Hartgrove, became interested, but he thought that surely Jesus would not say 'follow me' without making a way to do it. He read Bonhoeffer, and said goodbye to the American way of doing things – no 'cheap grace'. He described this as 'an epiphany moment'. In 2001 he married Leah, who had introduced him to the Simple Way. In 2003 he joined the Christian Peacemaker Teams in Baghdad as a ministry of presence against a war that the churches had called unjust. There he and Shane Claiborne of the the Simple Way Community were hurt in a car crash, and cared for by Iraqis at a hospital near a town named Rutba. These Iraqis showed them compassion even though they had recently lost loved ones in an American air strike. Jonathan, Leah and a friend decided to start a Christian community of hospitality, peacemaking and discipleship in the neighbourhood of Durham, North Carolina, an area broken by economic and racial fragmentation. They called it Rutba House. This group had many unanswered questions, so Jonathan secured a research grant, and called friends who had been interested in some fresh expression of radical Christianity to a meeting in a church opposite. The Houston *Catholic Worker* sponsored it, and the idea was also inspired by Alasdair MacIntyre's *After Virtue*,[20] in which he speaks of the fragmentation of the tradition of the West and the need 'for another Benedict'. The community at Rutba House called together a group of Anabaptists, Catholics, mainline Protestants and Evangelicals to discuss ways in which their lives could be understood and deepened as a neo-monastic movement. Their statement includes '12 Marks of a New Monasticism' which they hope will help to facilitate conversation about this movement of the Spirit:

Twelve Marks of a New Monasticism

Moved by God's Spirit we wish to acknowledge a movement of radical rebirth...A contemporary school for conversion which we have called a 'new monasticism', is producing a grassroots ecumenism and a prophetic witness within the North American Church which is diverse in form, but characterised by the following marks:

1. Relocation to abandoned places of empire

2. Sharing economic resources with fellow Community members and the needy among us

3. Hospitality to the stranger

4. Lament for racial divisions and active pursuit of a just reconciliation

5. Humble submission to Christ's Body, the Church

6. Intentional formation and a Community Rule

[20] MacIntyre, Alasdair (1997) *After Virtue*, Duckworth.

7. Nurturing common life amongst members of intentional community

8. Support for celibates, married couples and children

9. Geographical proximity to Community members

10. Care for the plot of God's earth given to us and supporting our local economies

11. Peacemaking in the midst of violence and conflict resolution

12. Commitment to a disciplined contemplative life

Following on from this they produced a Rutba House publishing venture which is printing as the New Monastic Library Series.[21]

The Catholic Worker

These impulses did not come out of the blue. Many of these young people had been inspired by the work of Dorothy Day, who founded the newspaper *The Catholic Worker* in 1935. This expressed dissatisfaction with the social order and took the side of labour unions, but its vision of the ideal future challenged both urbanisation and industrialism. It wasn't only radical but religious. The paper didn't merely complain but called on its readers to make personal responses. For the first half year *The Catholic Worker* was only a newspaper, but as winter approached, homeless people began to knock on the door. Essays by a contributor named Maurin called for renewal of the ancient Christian practice of hospitality to those who were homeless. In this way followers of Christ could respond to Jesus' words: 'I was a stranger and you took me in.' Maurin opposed the idea that Christians should take care only of their friends and leave care of strangers to impersonal charitable

[21] See www.newmonasticism.org

agencies. Every home should have its 'Christ Room' and every parish a house of hospitality ready to receive the 'ambassadors of God.'

Surrounded by people in need and attracting volunteers excited about ideas they had discovered in *The Catholic Worker*, Dorothy Day's apartment was the seed of many houses of hospitality to come. By the wintertime, an apartment was rented with space for ten women, soon after a place for men. Next came a house in Greenwich Village. In 1936 the community moved into two buildings in Chinatown, but no enlargement could possibly find room for all those in need. Mainly they were men. Dorothy Day wrote,

> ... grey men, the colour of lifeless trees and bushes and
> winter soil, who had in them as yet none of the green
> of hope, the rising sap of faith.

Many were surprised that, in contrast with most charitable centres, no one at The Catholic Worker set about reforming them. A crucifix on the wall was the only unmistakable evidence of the faith of those welcoming them. The staff received only food, board and occasional pocket money. The Catholic Worker became a national movement. By 1936 there were 33 Catholic Worker houses spread across the country. Due to the Depression, there were plenty of people needing them. The Catholic Worker also experimented with farming communes. In 1935 a house with a garden was rented on Staten Island. Soon after came Mary Farm in Easton, Pennsylvania, a property finally given up because of strife within the community. Another farm was purchased in upstate New York near Newburgh. Called the Maryfarm Retreat House, it was destined for a longer life. Later came the Maurin Peter Farm. Dorothy Day came to see the vocation of The Catholic Worker was not so much to found model agricultural communities as rural houses of hospitality.[22]

Shane Claiborne, founder of the Simple Way Community, Philadelphia, believes that the power of monasticism is a fusion of orthodoxy (right belief) with orthoprax (right action). His book *The Irresistible Revolution* describes how he has given up status and material possessions in order to radically serve Jesus among the poor.[23]

Scott Bessenecker, director of global projects with InterVarsity Christian Fellowship USA, begins his book *The New Friars*[24] with a visit to a traditional Franciscan Friary where the brothers smoked, swore and indulged: 'Underneath the austere Franciscan robe, tied with the simplicity of a rope belt, was a rich kid who simply got around the vow of poverty by enjoying someone else's wealth.' That friary closed, and was not, I hope, typical. But it makes his point. The people he calls the new friars come from a fresh generation 'who are begging someone to set the bar higher, to call them to uncommon levels of commitment and devotion'. They are often Protestants who, like Bessenecker, think that when Martin Luther left his monastic order and condemned the making of vows, he may have left the Protestant movement bereft of God-ordained 'focused communities of men and women with defined, disciplined devotion and a particular mission'.

Bessenecker regards new monastics who go to abandoned places in the USA, where 'the poor and homeless find freedom from the pains of want, and the middle-class and rich find freedom from the dangers of excess' the cousins of the new friars who go to slums in the developing world.

---

[22] Forest, Jim (1994) *Love is the Measure: a biography of Dorothy Day*, Orbis.

[23] Claiborne, Shane (2006) *The Irresistible Revolution*, Zondervan.

[24] Bessenecker, Scott (2006) *The New Friars*, IVP

Fifth wave – new expressions

24-7

In 1999 a prayer movement was birthed in Britain called 24-7. Young people gathered to create a monastery for a week, and maintained prayer, by rota, for twenty-four hours each day. Using the internet this movement spread worldwide. The experience was so powerful that people asked how they could take the basic idea forward in a sustainable way. As a result 'boiler rooms' were established in British towns such as Reading and Manchester, and then in the USA. The movement describes these as houses of prayer, mission, art and pilgrimage modelled on the ancient Celtic Christian communities and sometimes described as *Millennium 3* monasteries. Both the Reading and the Manchester boiler rooms had the blessing of the local bishop and attracted a great deal of media interest. The boiler room in Reading received a Government grant in recognition of the effectiveness of its work amongst young people excluded from school. More than twenty other locations asked for similar initiatives.[25]

Then, while Pete Greig was in the shower at the gym, he felt God saying that he wanted the 24-7 vision to be a springboard for something new. His thoughts turned to the eighteenth-century vow of Count Ludwig Nicklaus von Zinzendorf – the simple and remarkable Rule of his Honourable Order of the Mustard Seed in nineteenth-century Germany. Members of this Order wore a ring inscribed with the motto, 'None live for themselves', and solemnly pledged: to be true to Christ; to be kind to people; to take the Gospel to the nations. Pete introduced the idea of making vows to 24-7 people. In this he puts forward a 'trailer' for adopting a Rule of Life:

[25] Greig, Pete & Roberts, Dave (2004) *Red Moon Rising*, Kingsway Publications.

> Rules of Life can provide us with the ABC for a deeper walk with God: *Authentic* – a Rule helps us to live consistently with our convictions ... *Balanced* – a Rule helps us develop a balanced, sustainable, and enjoyable rhythm of life ... *Centred* – a Rule calls us back continually to the place of prayer ...

Instead of offering a Rule, Pete invites 24-7 enthusiasts to find a facilitator, band together with those whom the ancient Celts called the *cymbrogi*, the 'companions of the heart', and make a vow that is unique to them.[26]

If ever there was an expression of monasticism that can be called 'casting your bread upon the waters', this is it. *The Vision and the Vow* was followed in 2007 by *Punk Monk*, co-authored with Andy Freeman. This is a contribution to the spiritual formation of those who embark on a voyage of a vow, and introduces them to examples of communities of people with vows, from the Irish monasteries to Count Zinzendorf's village. It teaches the ancient art of breathing prayer, and gives guidance on the practice of learning, hospitality, and sustaining a boiler room.[27]

The Eden Project

The Eden Project recruits young people to work on the streets in a needy area of Britain. Typically they are financed by business and friends and hosted by a church. They take a four-year vow and live in groups of four.[28]

---

[26] Greig, Pete (2004) *The Vision and the Vow*, Kingsway Publications.

[27] Freeman, Andy & Greig, Pete (2007) *Punk Monk: New Monasticism and the Ancient Art of Breathing*, Regal.

[28] Willey, Eldred (ed) (2001)*Prayers of New Communities*, DLT – includes introductions as well as prayers from over 20 new UK communities.

Monos

The interest in new monasticism is reflected in networks such as Monos that make it a focus of study. Anthony Gormley, who began the Monos website writes:

> Over the last few decades, within the Christian Church and broader society, there has been an explosion in interest concerning the benefits and fruits of monastic spirituality and culture in both its historical and contemporary context. Fuelled by a deep human concern for spirituality, it has been suggested that we are in the middle of the development of a Christian dispersed sub-culture called Secular, Neo, New, Re, Domestic or Worldly Monasticism.
>
> Monos has been formed amidst this interest, as an attempt to offer a facility for the ongoing dialogue between monastic spirituality, society, culture and church.
>
> Monastic spirituality and culture, expressed through a lived Christian experience and academic reflection, is at the heart of what Monos is offering through its educational programme. To this end, Monos is working closely with the University of Wales Lampeter and their monastic studies programme and a number of traditional and new monastic communities.

Secular monastic communities

Another dimension of what might be called 'secular monastic life' began to grow through the Danish cohousing movement. This began in the 1980s and most of the communities still exist. These are based upon a multi-unit dwelling in which all residents have their own private unit, along with a common building that typically includes a dining hall which serves several common meals a week, a laundry, a childen's play area, and a garden. The cohousing movement has since taken off in the USA and has its own journal, *CoHousing*, and a website, www.cohousing.org. I was stirred by a workshop in Melbourne led by USA pioneers Tom and Christine Sine, who have done much to translate the cohousing model into a Christian context. Tom is a futures consultant to many Christian communities and his recent book *Mustard Seed vs McWorld* (published in 1999 by Baker Books, Grand Rapids) treats the role of the Church in the emerging global culture. The Sines have helped to establish a mission group of five families and one single person which, after studying various co-housing models, purchased a quarter acre of land near their church (Rockbridge, Oakland) and sought to find a new way to be church to a multi-cultural neighbourhood. This is now named the Temescal Cohousing Project. Around the edge are clusters of buildings. In the centre is a large common green. An old barn has become the young people's space. Residents have several common meals each week in the dining room, above which are residences. Sharing the street is an old farmhouse which residents have turned into a transition home for families coming off welfare. They are turning their land into an earth-friendly zone. Theirs is a heroic attempt to offer an alternative lifestyle to greed-fuelled capitalism. In the accounts I have read, however, I have seen no reference to common rhythms of prayer, and this, for me, raises a question mark.

These new expressions of monasticism have a wide appeal, but certain Church traditions have such a strong antipathy to anything that was thrown out at the Reformation that they fight shy of a term such as monasticism that brings negative perceptions to the fore. Yet Presbyterians, along with others, have been challenged by one of their lights, Eugene Peterson to rethink. He has called on Protestant church leaders to replace their 'ego lust to be God' with a corporate pattern that makes space for God. He writes:

Historically the most conspicuous corporate construction that does this is the monastery . . . The genius of the monastery is its comprehensiveness; all the hours of the day are defined by prayer; all the activity of the monks is understood as prayer . . . This external comprehensiveness penetrates community and soul.

He quotes Oxford historian Herbert Butterfield:

Sometimes I wonder at dead of night whether, during the next fifty years, Protestantism may not be at a disadvantage because a few centuries ago, it decided to get rid of monks.

Peterson calls for 'an open monastery', and concludes:

What is critical is an imagination large enough to contain all of life, all worship and work in prayer set in a structure adequate to the actual conditions in which it is lived out.[29]

New monasticism is untested. It remains to be seen whether it will be any more sustainable than were the charismatic communities of the 1970s. It therefore seems sensible to take a fresh look at old monasticism, to see whether it can throw light on the monastic quest today

[29] Peterson, Eugene (1992) *Under the Unpredictable Plant: An Exploration in Vocational Holiness*, Erdmans.

CHAPTER 2

Light for today from the old monasticism

It could be argued that the discovery of monasticism among Protestants is more a new discovery than a new monasticism. Most Reformers identified monasticism with the abuses of the late medieval period such as lavish lifestyle, the unbiblical assumption that celibate orders were superior, or the military orders used in the anti-Muslim crusades. It is now being recognised that these bad examples of monasticism were not typical of monasticism in all times and places.

Although some aspects of the new monasticism may, in fact, be new, other aspects may only seem to be new because the structured western Orders are taken to be the only monastic model. Even those Orders, after a two-hundred-year period, have often needed reform or they have died. Some of the earlier, more fluid forms of monasticism may resonate more with post-modern people.

What follows is not a systematic examination of monasticism (studies of these abound), but an attempt to point to the diversity of rays, some of which seem to me to throw light on our present search.

The Old Testament

The prophet Elijah lived from time to time as a hermit on the top of Mount Carmel, but he came down regularly to visit cities of Palestine where he upset the status quo and opened the way of love for God to come. Schools of prophets emerged in desert areas, for example, 2 Kings 2 and 6:1–5. This is one of the original impulses for monasticism, but over the centuries it got over-institutionalised, and it lost its wildness, spontaneity and cutting edge. There were Nazirites, a body of Israelites specially consecrated to God's service who fasted and abstained from alcohol, haircuts and contact with a dead person (Numbers 6; Jeremiah 35). At first they took life vows (cf. Samson, Judges 13:7) but later it was limited to a definite period. The apostle Paul joined with some Christians who were completing their Nazirite vows at Jerusalem (Acts 18:18; 21:23–26). Rechabites were founded by Rechab's son Jehonadab to live a simple, no-madic lifestyle as an alternative to the greedy possessiveness which had become the hallmark of their society (2 Kings 10). John the Forerunner, who lived for years in the desert where there were many Jewish communities such as the Essenes, may have related to one or more of these.

New Testament

In Egypt the Holy Family is believed to have wandered through the Nile delta region, and proceeded into the wastes of the Wadi Natrun to visit the monasteries there, then to have trekked back to old Cairo in order to embark south along the river Nile, before journeying inland to the monastery of Al-Muharraq near Luxor. James Cowan observes:

> Christ needed to be a product of a journey, a spiritual trek, through the hinterland of some primary experience that was Egypt.[30]

In the New Testament and the period following some Christians decided to live the Christian life in groups. The first Christians

[30] Cowan, James (2002) *Journey to the Inner Mountain*, Hodder & Stoughton.

in Jerusalem did this (Acts 2:44–47). It seems some widows became a kind of order with vows of celibacy (1 Timothy 5:3–6).

The New Testament churches were not mere house churches, they were often extended households with courtyards and guest accommodation and even a work area. An archeological floor plan of the first-century house of the apostle Peter in Capernaum[31] reveals that this was on the main road, and had several courtyards, accommodation for the owner, and quarters for family and friends. This house is widely associated with Peter and believed to be his although we cannot be certain.

At this house Peter's mother-in-law lived. Archeologists have discovered one room that was venerated by Christians from the second to the fourth centuries. This is probably where the church of Capernaum met and, it has been conjectured, is an extension of the room in which Jesus stayed when he lived in Capernaum. Here, the roof was broken and a man was lowered to be healed by Jesus.

Groups emerged on the edges of towns. In AD 107 Ignatius, Bishop of Antioch, wrote to a convent of virgins. The universal church's Council of Chalcedon in AD 154 laid down guidelines for monks and how bishops should relate to them.

Desert monasticism

As Christianity became a favoured, and then a nominal religion, in the fourth century some Christians who sought to follow Jesus in the simplicity of the Gospels emigrated into the Egyptian deserts. Three types of desert monk emerged. First, those who lived under one roof, with one rule and one abbot in organised monasteries, such as those founded by Pachomius in the south of Egypt. Second, hermits who lived solitary lives

[31] See V. Corbo, *Cafarnao*

removed from other people. Third, hermits, including some who were married, who lived in proximity to others whom they would visit for fellowship or oversight.

Pachomius' monks were divided into houses according to the craft they practised, such as agriculture, tailoring and baking. Their rule influenced those of Basil and Benedict. The first solitary hermit was Paul of Thebes (d. 353) whose life was recorded by Jerome. Then came Antony whose *Life*, written by Bishop Athanasius, has inspired countless hermits ever since. Then there was the third expression of desert monasticism, whose appeal is reviving today. Hermits who lived independently, but in the same desert locality, gathered together at weekends for shared worship and food. They were responsible for their own work, welfare and timetable, but they mostly followed the Rule of the pioneer hermit who had drawn them to come. Such communities flourished in the desert at Nitria, Cellia, and at Scetis, which gave its name (skete) to this third way.

The aim of many desert Christians was to flee from every thing that distracted them from living for God alone. A famous saying was: 'The one who abides in solitude and is quiet, is delivered from fighting three battles – those of hearing, speech, and sight. Then that person will have but one battle to fight – the battle of the heart.' The aim was that nothing but love for God and neighbour would be left. But the heart was a battleground. Eight destructive passions were identified by teachers such as Evagrius Ponticus: Gluttony, lust, acquisitiveness, complaining, temper, restless boredom, love of flattery, and pride. Ceaseless struggle against these was essential. This struggle included transparent sharing of all thoughts with a spiritual elder.

Ever since that particular experiment, which was cut short by barbarian invasions, some people have tried to create 'deserts' in countries of very different climate, either as solitaries or as sketes. Joceline's *Life of Kentigern* states that 'after the fusion of the Primitive Church under the apostles and their successors ... they dwelt alone, as did St Kentigern himself, in single cottages from the time when they had become mature in age and doctrine.'[32]

David Adam writes:

> If the desert is a place of pruning, it is a pruning that life may blossom and grow in the right direction ... The desert is the place where they sought to live life in the depths and in a constant relationship with the ever-present God.[33]

Can desert monasticism be for us a source of inspiration or negativity? The truth perhaps lies somewhere between the two following evaluations:

> Their cells in the hills were like tents filled with divine choirs – people chanting, studying, fasting, praying, rejoicing in the hope of future boons, working for the distribution of alms, and maintaining love and harmony among themselves. It was as if one truly looked on a land all its own – a land of devotion and righteousness. For neither perpetrator nor victim of injustice was there, nor complaint.[34]
>
> There is perhaps no phase in the moral history of mankind of a deeper or more painful interest than this ascetic epidemic. A hideous, distorted and emaciated maniac, without knowledge, without patriotism, with-

[32] Macdonald, Iain (ed) (1993) *Saint Mungo*, Floris. Saint Mungo was also known as Kentigern.

[33] Adam, David (2000) *A Desert in the Ocean: the spiritual journey according to St Brendan the Navigator*, Triangle.

[34] Athanasius, *The Life of Antony* (Early Christian Lives), Penguin Classics (1998).

out natural affection, spending his life in a long routine of useless and atrocious self-torture, and quailing before the ghastly phantoms of his delirious brain, had become the ideal of the nations which had known the writings of Plato and Cicero and the *Lives* of Socrates and Cato.[35]

Cappadocia (modern Turkey) fourth–sixth centuries

Here the monastic tradition took a major new turn through Basil who became the great Bishop of Caesarea. Basil developed communal monasticism with a household feel. The Cappadocian and other fathers of the Eastern Church did not treat fourth-century monasticism as a special form of Christian life, but as the actualisation of what in principle was a life demanded of all Christians.[36] Basil's mother and his sister Macrina moved to a house on the banks of the River Iris, near their family home at Annesi and founded a community there. Macrina established a kind of fourth-century family monastery. Her mother taught her the scriptures, household management, spinning and weaving. After her fiancé died, when she was twelve, she decided to become Christ's bride for ever. As the eldest of ten children, she influenced Basil to give his life to God.

Basil came back from university 'puffed up with the pride of oratory'. Macrina took him in hand with such effect that he gave up his property and possessions and became a monk. Another of Macrina's brothers, the clever and handsome Naucratius, became a hermit and supported the poor through

[35] Willian Lecky quoted in Waddell, Helen (translated and introduced) (1998) *The Desert Fathers*, Vintage. William Lecky (1838–1903), an Anglo-Irish historian and essayist of classic Whig proclivities, was perhaps the greatest historical scholar Ireland had ever produced.

[36] Greer, R. A. (1986) *Broken Lights and Mended Lives*, Pennsylvania State University Press.

fishing expeditions. Her other brother Gregory, who married, became a great teacher and wrote her *Life*. They encouraged Basil to live in a hermitage on the opposite bank of the River Iris. Soon this too resembled a monastery, and solitaries came to live nearby. Here Basil wrote his two sets of *Rules*. Basil saw his revival of community as restoring the way that Christ's first apostles lived.

It was often the monastics who upheld what is now taught as Orthodox Christianity, as against a large part of the church, which, in the controversy over the interpretation of the Trinity, for example, went over to the Arian heresy. A conclusion some draw from this is that a church with rich monastic roots is a healthier church.

Basil's monasteries had a welcome for married people and children. They sometimes adopted orphans. They were housed separately but prayed together. From the beginning eastern monasticism was thought of as a movement for women and children as well as for men. In fact, the skeptic Gibbon, in sneering at it in his book *The History of the Decline and Fall of the Roman Empire* says that the monastic movement was recruited from 'millions of either sex, of every age and of every rank' (Chapter 37).[37]

Basil became 'the father of Eastern monasticism'.[38] In the fourth century monasticism was permanently established in Constantinople. By the mid-century there were over 100 monasteries in that city and the capital city of Chalcedony across the water. The Council of Chalcedon in AD 451 placed monasteries under the supervision of a bishop. Church regulations for monasteries were confirmed by those of the state under the Christian Emperor Justinian. These were based upon Basil's rules. A key issue was how to reduce overload of the

---

[37] *The History of the Decline and Fall of the Roman Empire* was originally published in six volumes between 1776 and 1788.

[38] Morison, E. F. (1912) *St Basil and His Rule: a study in early monasticism*, OUP.

abbot and to prevent him becoming a burned-out bureaucrat. St Theodore, founder of the ninth-century monasteries which became known as Studdites, divided the responsibilities of the monasteries, rather like the house system in a large British public school.

Nestorians

In AD 635 some radical eastern monks sent Alopen to China. That mission spread across the land. A monument dug up by workmen near Xi'an in 1623 commemorated more than one hundred years of missionary monks and nuns, proclaiming that Christianity:

> '. . . was helpful to all creatures and beneficial to all men. So let it have free course throughout the empire.' The Nestorian missionary schools prepared them in medicine, agriculture and theology.[39]

Celtic People's monastic churches

The Irish monastic settlements were the earliest forms of towns. Some of them were islands. The *Life of Brendan*, perhaps written as early as AD 800, recalls his sixth-century visit to an island of monks:

> When we reached the island the brothers came to us out of their cells, like a swarm of bees; and though their dwellings were separate from one another, there was no division in their converse, or counsel, or affection. And their only victuals were apples and nuts, and roots of such kinds of herbs as they found. And the brothers

[39] Wallis Budge, E. A. (trs) (1928) *The Monks of Kublai Khan, Emperor of China* by Rabban Bar Sauma, The Religious Tract Society.

used to go to their separate cells from Compline until cockcrow.[40]

Glendalough, which nestles between the Wicklow mountains, is probably the world's best preserved Celtic monastic city. The holy life of Saint Kevin, who in the sixth century established a hidden hermitage near the Upper Lake, attracted many to live nearby after his death. Many of its remains date back to the tenth century. In the inner area the celibate monks lived, prayed, studied and offered hospitality. The large cross was probably the focus of the teaching centre. The scriptorium is where the monks transcribed, illuminated with artistic designs and put covers on the Scriptures. Precious stones such as lapis lazuli were imported from as far as Afghanistan. In the outer area the married members of the monastic village lived. Here there would have been the tannery, the farming, and later metal-work and other crafts.

In answer to the question 'What was a monastery in early Ireland?' a panel in the museum at Devenish Island gave the following answer:

A monastery is:

A focus for worship:
'Let him be constant at prayer, his canonical hours let him not forget them.'

A centre for scholarship and craftsmanship:
'My hand is weary with writing ... my slender-beaked pen pours forth a black draught of shining dark-blue ink.'

A holy place of burial:

---

[40] O'Donaghue, Denis (1994) *Lives and Legends of Saint Brendan the Voyager*, Llanerch facsimile.

'Be the earth that covers me. Holy earth of monastery
I lying there alone.'

A place where many people lived:
'Multitudinous Devenish.'

An economic unit:
'Three sounds of increase: the lowing of a cow in milk,
the din of a smithy and the swish of a plough.'

A place where guests were received:
'A clean house for guests and a big fire, washing and
bathing for them, and a couch without sorrow.'

Where children were educated:
'Whence are you, learning's son?
From Clonmacnois I come,
My course of studies done.'

Where produce and treasures from the surrounding
land were stored:
'The church at Duleek was broken into by Vikings and
its fill of prosperity was taken out of it' (in AD 881).

A sanctuary for fugitives:
'Molaise (St) is no weak protection for me.'

A place where meetings were held:
'Devenish of Assemblies.'

*(Copied from a panel in the museum on Devenish
Island.)*

The Danish invasions and local hostility practically banished
monastic life from Britain until Dunstan (AD 908–88). He lived
as a hermit near Glastonbury and practised the crafts of painting, embroidery and metalwork. After being made Abbot of
Glastonbury and then Archbishop of Canterbury he instituted

a re-enlivened monasticism which embraced musical experiments and creative arts.

Western Orders

The Rule of St Benedict (died AD 550) brought order and stability into monasticism. He is thought of by many as the father of western monasticism. His rule was adopted by most western monasteries during the seventh and eighth centuries. Each local monastery became part of an Order. Local distinctives diminished, monks were forbidden to 'wander'. Monasticism in the west has ever since largely consisted of Orders, based on Benedict's Rule, or revised versions of it, with some new ones.

These Orders include:

Augustinians – these began in eleventh-century Italy as communities of clergy who kept a little-known Rule written by Augustine of Hippo in the fifth century.

Carmelites – founded in 1154 by Berthold, these mendicants claim continuity with hermits who settled on Mount Carmel since the time of Elijah. Silence and contemplation are foundational.

Carthusians – founded by Bruno in 1084. The monks are vowed to silence.

Cistercians – founded in 1098 at Citeaux as a reformed, stricter form of Benedictine Order.

The Benedictine Monastery at Worth, in England, attracted worldwide attention through the acclaimed BBC TV series

Monastery, when six decidedly unmonastic members of the public agreed to live there for a period and engage with the monks. It became a transforming experience for each of them.[41]

Mendicant Friars

Saint Francis established The Order of Friars Minor in 1209. With their love of poverty and spontaneity, the Franciscan movement has brought colour and compassion into many a market place. Unlike monastics, these are travelling mendicants with a vow of poverty. Dominicans – founded by Saint Dominic in the 1220s – are teaching and preaching friars.

Mount Athos' four types of monk

In the tenth century the focus of monasticism shifted to Greece. A combination of the three different forms of monasticism for males only (the solitary, the residential community and the loose association under a spiritual guide) was introduced in the mountain peninsular known as Mount Athos. There, monks who have been tested in residential community may move out into solitary cells. In the fourteenth century these solitaries were given the name Hesychasts. In the fifteenth century a fourth form of monasticism developed on Mount Athos; known as idiorrhythism, the word means roughly 'living in one's own way.' The monk receives a small allowance, may earn his own keep and live elsewhere in his own property, but returns once a year to the parent monastery to give account to the Abbot for his Rule of Life.

Currently the 'Black Beards' (e.g. young recruits from the USA) are replacing the 'White Beards' (old traditionalists from Europe) on Mount Athos. Archimandrite Vasileios, Abbot of

[41] Jamieson, Christopher (2006) *Sanctuary: monastic steps for everyday life,* Weidenfeld & Nicolson.

Iveron Monastery, Mount Athos, has issued a booklet for young people.[42] He writes, 'Stillness, hesychia, is a great revolution.' He reminds young people that a monk not only lives for God alone; a monk, as St Antony said, must always reach out to others. He challenges the myth that solitaries are escapists. Quoting Abba Isaac, he says that the more a person flees from worldly distractions the more people want to be with that person. It is the egotist, who boasts about self and disparages others, who repels people and lives in true loneliness, in hell. Monasteries are not defined by the work they do, or the form of organisation, but by the experience of living so that from the depths of each monk bursts the words 'Glory to God that I am human'. In this way the ideal monk, he says, is the person who has become perfectly natural, completely themselves, with a fire within. It follows there is movement and flexibility. If a monk feels called to be married, or to move elsewhere, or to get a job in the outside world, he shares that with his spiritual father in transparency. If he gets their blessing, nothing is lost, everything is gain.

Father Sophrony was born in Russia in 1896 and trained as an artist. After the Revolution he migrated to Paris. He became a monk at Mount Athos, Greece, where he befriended the honoured Staretz Silouan, who became his spiritual guide. He became a priest and was elected spiritual confessor by several of the Mount Athos communities. In 1959 he moved to Britain with several friends and received people from all walks of life for spiritual direction at the Community at Tolleshunt Knights, Essex, which he founded. Two hallmarks of Father Sophrony and this Community are the constant use of the Jesus Prayer as the focus of liturgy, and the cultivation of an attitude of mercy and freedom from prejudice towards all people.

---

[42] *The Christian in a Changing World: Monasticism and the New Realities of Life* Alexander Press, Kontral (1997).

Monastic groups in Russia

Monasticism has played a pivotal role in Russia. The monk Sergius, who advised Russian rulers at the time of the Tartar invasion in the thirteenth century, is regarded as the builder of 'Holy Russia', whose identity has ever since been linked with monasticism. The solitary (for example the staretz) and skete forms of monasticism never wholly died away in the Orthodox east, and at times they have strongly resurfaced. The region of great monasteries such as Zagorsk, Optina and Valaam is named 'The Northern Thebaid' after the Thebes area of Egypt where Pachomius established monasticism. The St Herman of Alaska Brotherhood publish a series on the elders of the Optina Skete from 1841 to 1996.[43]

I recently visited a series of Russian monasteries which became almost shells under Communist rule but which are now fast reviving, albeit often with money from the state for major rebuilding programmes. Young people, whose parents often remain atheists, are taking vows in monasteries such as Pskov and Valaam. At Valaam I was informed that the abbot seeks to enlarge the library to include spiritual works in English.

Apostolic Orders

This term is used by Catholics to describe the many Orders which engage in active outreach. Many of these started after the Counter-Reformation (sixteenth – seventeenth centuries) and up to the last century. Mother Teresa's Missionary Sisters of Mercy is perhaps the most widely known and respected Apostolic Order. These orders are more committed to action and not necessarily tied to geography. This is in contrast to 'monastic orders' where monks are committed to a life of

---

[43] The Optina Elders Series in 8 volumes published by St Hermon Press, 10 Beegum Gorge Road, PO Box 70, Plantina, California 96076.

contemplation in a specific geography or monastery and are defined as enclosed communities.

Anglican communities

The Anglican/Episcopal Communion currently has 995 men and 1420 women in some 93 communities. Older communities such as the Community of the Resurrection, the Society for Sacred Mission, the Society of St Francis, and the Society of John the Evangelist tend to be aging. In Australasia and the Pacific however, there are more members than in all the other continents combined. The Melanesian Brotherhood consist of young men who look like rugby players. They take vows of poverty, celibacy and obedience for five years only. During that time they live like brothers among the people, sharing in their harvests and heartaches, and becoming peacemakers.

Protestant experiments

Although most Protestant church streams rejected monasteries, some, such as the Mennonites and the Moravians, established intentional communities. Count Ludwig von Zinzendorf, like early Irish clan leaders, offered his prime German estate for God's work. To Berthelsdorf in 1722 flocked Moravian refugees. They formed a community of thirty-two houses and drew up a covenant for Christian living. The Bruderhof communities thrive today.

Catholic experiments

A Carmelite told me that charismatic renewal touched many monasteries in the 1970s and 1980s, and that many monks who experienced spiritual renewal left the Order because they could live renewed lives better outside than inside. Other Carmelites, however, sought to renew the Order. The Benedictine Weston

Priory, in New England, USA, decided to ask the question 'Does this bring life?'. Decisions about who should become novices, what worship styles and work projects should be pursued are made in the light of that question.

Passionist sisters of the new Green Mountain Monastery in the USA have been inspired by the creationist spirituality of Fr Thomas Berry. Their liturgies reflect the 'unfolding earth story' and their work includes sustainable farming. They seek to create the first 'ecozoic monastery' and to model 'earth healing' that will bring about an 'Ecozoic era'. When I visited them they were working to get their liturgies approved by the Vatican.[44]

Despite these exceptional examples, and the comparative popularity of a Benedictine Community such as Ampleforth, Yorkshire, the trend in traditional monasteries in the west is towards sharp decline.

Lessons from the failures of old monasticism

A Roman Catholic Diocesan spokesman has said 'We don't believe in the new monasticism, we believe in monasticism, full stop.' It is easy, and cheap, to contrast the latest excitements of the new monasticism with the failures of some old monasticism. Nevertheless, failures there were.

At the time of the sixteenth-century European Reformation, which abolished the monasteries, the main arguments against them were that power had corrupted them and made them mistreat the people. They had created a 'them and us' approach (the superior Christians were celibate monks and everyone else was 'them') which was unsuited to the introduction of the printed Bible to all people, and to its teaching of 'the priesthood of all believers'.[45]

[44] See www.greenmountainmonastery.org
[45] The priesthood of all believers is the biblical teaching that every Christian, because they are 'in Christ', share in his priestly work. Thus the apostle Peter described all Christians as 'a royal priesthood' (1 Peter 2:9).

Monasteries were perceived to extoll 'poverty' for aristocrats who were well-looked after in the monasteries, but who had no concern for the people outside for whom poverty was an all too real curse, not a blessing. They extolled celibacy in such a way that sex and marriage were devalued as second class. They enforced obedience in such a way that shy monastics became repressed and retarded as human beings. On the Holy Island of Lindisfarne, where I live, as in countless other places, the dissolved monasteries were so unpopular that the locals ransacked the buildings, and used their very stones to build houses for themselves.

The new monasticism transcends both the Protestant and Roman Catholic monastic frameworks which have dominated the Western Church since the Reformation. It also brings a more open, ecumenical attitude. Some of the churches arising out of the sixteenth-century Protestant / Catholic schism have been dogmatically separatist. They have seen themselves as the centre of reform and have tended to look down on others. True monasticism is grounded in a humility that has no such grandiose illusions. It has a deep connectedness which derives from a recognition that there is only one holy, catholic, orthodox, apostolic Church. Many of the new communities have Protestant as well as Catholic, and sometimes also Orthodox, members or make people of all faith backgrounds feel at home.

Postmodern Christians (those who start where people are and go with the flow of their patterns) who seek a new monasticism are wary of structures that are imposed from the centre; they do not want to be trapped in a new legalism; they don't want to be shut off from ordinary people. They see themselves as on a journey, and can't prejudge what they will be doing at a later stage of the journey. They want to be free to follow each prompting of the Spirit, to be single or to marry. Nevertheless, those who embrace new monasticism seek to be connected to the self-emptying God in the centre and in the streets, in the other parts of the Body of Christ and in their own hearts. They would be wise, therefore, to bear in mind insights of people such as the missionary statesman Ralph Winter. He suggests that the Church experiences unprecedented growth about every four hundred years. Drawing from Latourette's *A History of Christianity* he identifies five critical renaissances:

- The Classical renaissance (AD 400)
  Celtic and Augustinian monks.

- The Carolingian renaissance (AD 800)
  Benedictine and Nestorian monks.

- The Medieval renaissance (AD 1200)
  Franciscans and Dominicans.

- The Reformation and Counter-Reformation (AD 1600)
  Jesuits, Moravians and Anabaptists.

- The Evangelical renaissance which he believes is
  beginning now.[46]

New monastics would also do well to heed these words of the eminent Protestant church historian Adolph Harnack, who said:

It was always the monks who saved the Church when sinking, emancipated her when becoming enslaved to the world, defended her when assailed. These it was that kindled hearts that were growing cold, bridled refractory spirits, recovered for the Church alienated nations.[47]

---

[46] Winter, Ralph D. & Hawthorne, Steen C. (ed) (1981) *The Kingdom Strikes Back: Ten Epochs of Redemptive History in Perspectives on the World Christian Movement: A Reader* Pasadena, California.

[47] Harnack, Adolph (1901) *Monasticism: Its Ideals and History*, Williams & Norgate as quoted in *Re-Monking the Church: A Lutheran Appraisal of Monastic Spirituality and Structures of Mission* Charles Lindquist (Unpublished thesis, Fuller Theological Seminary 1989)

CHAPTER 3

Hard questions for new monastics

If the aspirations of new monastics are not to crumble, hard questions need to be asked and addressed. These are some questions I have been asked, and some provisional thoughts in response.

How could we grow a 'new' monastery in a city?

Five essentials are:

1. A core who accept a Rule, covenant or set of values.

2. A sufficient percentage of this core who live near each other.

3. A sufficient percentage who offer regular corporate prayer.

4. Some common work or focus.

5. An agreed way of making decisions.

How are non-institutional monks accountable?

Benedict rejected a type of monk (the Sarabite) who avoided the discipline of a Rule or a superior and who claimed that whatever he liked doing was holy.

The Community of Aidan and Hilda sets out a broad ethos in its Way of Life, and asks a voyager to account transparently to a reflective soul friend who is recognised by the wider church. The Community asks the soul friend to check out with the voyager how they apply the principles of simplicity, purity and obedience. We encourage the voyager to listen intently, with an attitude of submission to the voice of God in the soul friend. We encourage transparency in the revealing of thoughts in order that self-will may shrink and trust may grow. The Community now engages a would-be voyager in a process of self-appraisal, discernment and spiritual formation.

If new monastics are free to move on, how does one sustain community?

In a dispersed community, relationships are sustained through means such as communal web sharing, prayer diaries, visits, area meetings, annual retreats, financial giving, and written feedback. When members of a community are under one roof or join in a common undertaking, house rules are drawn up. For example, at our Retreat and Spirituality Centre on the Holy Island of Lindisfarne we all honour the times of corporate prayer, the guidelines for guests, the need for good communication and for a process of mutual discernment to be engaged in before any sudden move to somewhere else.

How can you combine 'framework' with 'flow'?

If we are to flourish, the framework we accept in common with our fellow new monastics must allow 'the garden of our unchosen lives' enough space to breathe and connect with its creative flow. We have not avoided the call of commitment, yet we remain true to God in our unrealised potential. We do not flee from complexity.

Are not rules a new form of legalism?

It is true that the idea of rules and regulations imposed from above does not appeal to Protestants nor to postmodern people generally, and that a Rule is essential to monasticism.

We start at the other end. We inwardly embrace love, and then work out how to give this consistent, practical expression. We distinguish between legalism and life-sustaining structure, which God has built into creation; and between self-centred individualism and the freedom that Christ promises. To develop a God-centred rhythm that is workable and holistic requires us to be practical and to include different aspects of life. In the Community of Aidan and Hilda the vows we take are understood as life-giving principles. As we work out how to apply them we ask 'Is this life-giving?'. Those things that are not life-giving we allow to die away. This is also why we adopt a Way, rather than a Rule of Life.

Evangelicals increasingly recognise the need for 'whole life discipling'. In his unpublished paper, *Changing Our Habits: a New Model of Monasticism for the Contemporary Church*, Matt Rees suggests we have a plan for five key areas of our lives. These are: how a person relaxes or looks after their body, how they do their work, how they make relationships, how they are involved in justice or ecology, how they develop themselves mentally. These are all discipleship issues that need to be provided for in a balanced, and therefore rhythmic, way.

If you change the vow of poverty don't you make a mockery of the monastic calling?

Most, but not all, traditional Religious Orders within Christianity require monks or nuns to make a vow of poverty. This usually means having no property, capital or other possessions. These may be sold and given away or to the monastery. Some monasteries return an amount of capital if a member withdraws and goes back to a secular life.

John Chrysostom, a fourth-century leader of the Eastern Church, wrote:

What are we to fear? The confiscation of our goods? 'We brought nothing into this world and we shall surely take nothing from it.' I have no fear of poverty, no desire for wealth.

In the new monasticism the generosity of God, not the lust for money, is regarded as the deepest reality we should move in. The love of money is certainly a root of all kinds of evils (1 Timothy 6:10) and it is certain, as Jesus taught, that human beings cannot serve both God and Money (Luke 16:3), but this false love of money is rooted in the desire to control. It is possible to choose poverty out of a false desire to have everything in our life controlled safely.

The Community of Aidan and Hilda's Way of Life states:

Simplicity means the willingness to be poor or rich for God according to God's direction. We resist the temptations to be greedy or possessive, and we will not manipulate people or creation for our own ends. We are bold to use all we have for God without fear of possible poverty. God's ultimate purpose for our lives is that we live for God's glory. God will give us everything there is if we can handle it for the Glory of God. It is as if God says to us, 'If it is my will, you can afford it. If it is not my will, you shouldn't want to afford it.'

There are different layers of character formation in relation to money. The bottom layer is to practice abstinence, to learn to do without. Some of us are so eaten up with the craving for money that we need to stay in that layer. But there is a higher stage in character formation. This is when our spirits are free to trust God for everything. When we are poor and in need, we discover streams of resource in the great God of all creation. These can be streams of enterprise, gifts, faith building and work patterns. In the Bible Joseph models for us how to move from one stage to another. He had to be brought into the poverty of a prison, and tested to see whether he would trust in God alone. When he passed that test he was trusted with the wealth of super-power Egypt.

The suggestion that we may be called to be rich has raised eyebrows. 'I do not think this is possible,' I have been told, 'for it is more difficult for a rich person to enter the kingdom of God than for a camel to go through the eye of a needle ... ' Yes, yet Jesus added 'But with God all things are possible.'

If our *aim* is to be rich, or if we are driven by the desire for riches then we cannot enter the kingdom of God. But if, like Abraham, we are called and are willing to leave all, and then are also promised a good material as well as spiritual inheritance, we are blessed indeed. There are billionaires who anonymously tithe 90 per cent of their income. They have truly put their riches at God's disposal.

A modern Rule may require us to give away money and possessions that are surplus to our true needs. What those needs are will differ for each person. The need for some things of beauty, or family heritage may be true needs for some people. The need to invest and multiply income for a clearly and commonly agreed God-given purpose may be a true need for others.

In practical terms, the new monastic keeps accounts of his income and expenditure and submits these to his or her soul friend. The soul friend is free to suggest increased alms giving, decreased consumption, or the pooling of some resources. In this way the delusion that any assets are ultimately ours is dispelled.

How can a married person be a monk?

The word monk comes from monos, which means one who is alone – surely this requires celibacy? And how can a person who has taken one life vow (marriage) then take another? The Church of England Advisory Council for Bishops and Religious Communities put this point to me. I replied that the Church has already agreed that a person can take two life vows, otherwise it would not allow monks to be ordained priests.

Old and new monastics alike dedicate themselves to live for God alone, in the sense of serving God above all and in the way they serve others. It has never meant that we jettison faithfulness in human relationships.

Nevertheless, I agree that there is danger in taking two life vows. A parish, which expects its shepherd to lay down her life for her sheep, can feel betrayed if their monk pastor is commanded to give priority time to the work of her Order. If a husband and wife are members of a Community, but come to a Community meeting with an agreed position on some matter, it destroys community.

I believe that a married person may become a monk if their spouse also makes vows or releases them to live by theirs; if both spouses treat the marriage itself as a form of monastery, in the sense of daily laying down their 'rights' in order to build up the other; if they heed this advice of Theodore the Studite (AD 759–826): 'Let your body and soul be divided equally in love among all your spiritual children and brothers.' So they make times to be alone, in order to be open to all.

What does a vow of purity mean?

It means we release each person to be as God wants them to be, and never feed off them in a way that robs some future partner of what belongs to that relationship alone. It means we resist the desire to treat people as sexual objects. For a single person it means abstaining from genital intercourse outside of a committed lifelong relationship. Genital intercourse is only one aspect of sexuality. Other aspects need to be developed in a non-demanding way: intimacy in friendship, touch, appreciation of beauty and physical attractiveness in other people and joy in deep flow of communication.

For married people the vow of faithfulness means monogamy. Within this, it means placing sexual urges in God's control; giving selves to the other for love of the other. It might also mean mutual restraint for the good of those they need to be fully available to, or for the worship of God.

What is the new monastic equivalent to the vow of obedience to a superior?

A vow of service. In western liberal society the highest good is often assumed to be the freedom to make choices without reference to any one else. Christians exercise the choice to voluntarily lay their lives down for others, to consider the effects of their choices on others, to allow individual decisions to be bound by the common good, to recognise the need for mutual accountability in the Body of Christ.

What's new about the new monasticism?

Monasticism always had to be born and take shape in the context of its time, and our time is different to any that has gone before. Postmodern people have instant access to information, can choose a series of careers or lifestyles within onelife time, have scientific knowledge of sexual and personal development, and so on. So we suggest these six new features:

1. Frameworks are more flexible

Routine is expendable if it inhibits God-given impulses to adventure. The core community does not have to turn up for everything. Routine as an end in itself clogs and ossifies. The postmodern monk always has an adventure. We should maximise flexi-time and reduce fixed corporate times to the minimum essentials. Traditional monasticism is struggling for breath because the monastic framework has become a boss, not a servant. This is sometimes justified in the name of obedience. It is good to a certain degree for the ego of a monk to have to fit into a framework that is not to his or her liking. The new monasticism is about mutual discerning of God's calling and gifting of each monk, and of how the framework can best enable these to be used for God's glory and the upbuilding of others. The issue for the new monastic framework is how can it avoid being a plaything of colliding egos? Part of the answer is to have agreed periods of listening and mutual accountability.

2. Leaders are mutually accountable

In the first two millennia obedience to the Abba is a fundamental requirement. This is healthy inasmuch as it spurs the monk to abandon self-will. However, if the Abba is blind or manipulative this violates the monks as well as God. The Abba himself needs to check out with someone. We suggest that the fully mature monks elect a group of wise, mature members who listen to God for the Abba and his decisions. Thus what we might call a presbyteral element is introduced into the monastery (In fact, Benedictines make big decisions like a closure of a school collectively.) In some new communities leaders are elected for a specified period.

3. Vows are multi-track

People are welcome to make vows of different kinds and different duration without it being assumed that some are 'better' than others. Within a monastery some may be celibate, and others married. Some may make trial vows, others make full vows for a specified period, and others take life vows. Families may live near a monastery and have a close relationship with it.

4. Disciplines are based on understanding of human development

The early desert Christians diminished the body to almost nothing in order to live in the spirit. Modern monastics neither idolise nor demonise the body. We aim that it should be 'as it was in the age of innocence'. So exercise and food that fuels it are good in as much as they service the body as a temple of the Holy Spirit, rather than for its own sake. We may replace a physical desert with a psychic desert. That is, we try to create a zone that is free from the eight destructive passions (gluttony, fornication, love of money, anger, sorrow, despondency, vainglory and pride).

5. There are not two tiers of 'ordinary' and 'monastic' people

In many, though not all, earlier periods of monasticism people from well-educated, wealthy backgrounds chose to enter a monastery. They had the social and work disciplines to make a go of monastic life. Although they gave up personal possessions, they had servants to do some of the chores. People from uneducated backgrounds could not have coped. The Franciscans bucked that trend, and today there is equal opportunity for all.

A vow is taken, or not taken, on the basis of a person's calling; it does not indicate that they are above anyone else in the heavenly stakes.

6. Local is global

A true monastic life is about being fully human, not necessarily about being set apart. A work of God in one local monastery can become yeast in the world more quickly than hitherto because of the global highway. We need monastic guidelines for the use of the web, that protect monks from data overload and ego trips yet enable monasteries to be globally aware and receptive.

Surely the 'Three Evangelical Counsels' have stood the test of time and should be inviolable?

For the few who make them, the vows of poverty, celibacy and obedience to a superior have indeed stood the test of time. One reason for this is that they address the three greatest human drives: money, sex and power. By adopting these vows many monks and nuns have been gloriously freed from enslavement to these drives. However, money, sex and power are also gifts, and many monks and nuns have also been enslaved by falsely denying them.

If these vows are taken as principles to be applied in ways that are appropriate to differing situations, they become relevant to us all. The traditional monasteries have applied these principles in a particular way. But as we have seen, there are other ways to apply them.

CHAPTER 4

The universal monk

I have pointed out that fourth-century Christian leaders like Athanasius, Basil the Great and John Chrysostom saw monasticism 'not as a special form of the Christian life but as the actualisation of what was in principle demanded of all Christians'.[48] Whilst Basil founded and organised monastic communities in the conventional sense, it is quite clear that writings like *The Longer Rules* are intended for the guidance of all Christians. Monasticism was, to borrow a recent political phrase, for the many and not just for the few.

St John Chrysostom wrote:

> The Holy Scriptures do not know of any such distinction (between a monk and a lay person). They enjoin that all lead the life of the monk, even if they are married and have children . . . The Holy Spirit demands the same rigorous observance as that demanded from monks.[49]

According to the Belgian scholar Archimandrite Boniface Luykx, Eastern monasticism presents 'a paradigm of true Christianity in the midst of a worldwide crisis of values', offering the genuine values 'that modern man needs in order to recover from his nihilism', and which are 'the backbone for

---

[48] Greer, R. A. (1986) *Broken Lights and Mended Lives*, Pennsylvania State University Press.

[49] Wagner, Sister Monica (1962) *Saint Basil, Ascetical Works, the Fathers of the Church* (vol. 9), The Catholic University of America Press, 223–337.

building up a new world.' These values, he stresses, are not mere wishes, for in the Eastern monasteries they have been lived out, 'not just perfunctorily, but charismatically, with joyful and creative commitment' (*Eastern Monasticism and the Future of the Church*, 1993, pp. 176-180), or, as Father Zosima puts it in Dostoyevsky's *Brothers Karamazov*, 'a monk is not a different kind of man, but merely such as all men on earth ought to be.'

Turning to Western Christianity, Ian Bradley has persuasively argued that:

> ... for Christians living in the British Isles between the fifth and eleventh centuries, the monastery rather than the parish church was the primary focus for worship, pastoral care, and religious instruction.[50]

Here, it seems, monasticism was in some sense for all. Even as brief a historical survey as this highlights some fascinating questions. Would it be beneficial to revive the Eastern and Celtic model of monasticism as the normal Christian life, and would it be possible to do so?[51]

Raimundo Panikar in his book *Blessed Simplicity: The Monk as Universal Archetype*[52] views the monk as an element that is in every person. Since his youth he has seen himself as a monk without a monastery, or at least without walls other than those of the entire planet. He defines the monk as a person who so desires to reach the ultimate that he renounces all that distracts

[50] Bradley, Ian (2000) *Colonies of Heaven: Celtic Models for Today's Church*, Darton, Longman & Todd.

[51] See the Appendix: 'Followers of the Way: Biblical foundations for monastic living', a paper by Simon Reed, St John's College, Durham at the Community of Aidan and Hilda's summer school on the new monasticism, July 2007.

[52] Panikar, Raimundo (1982) *Blessed Simplicity: The Monk as Universal Archetype*, Seabury Press.

from this. With this definition, monkhood cannot find its fullest expression in an institution that puts achievement of a common task above the working of God in the individual monk. Panikar sees many traditional monasteries as such organisations. The monastery he calls for is an organism, which requires the harmonious interaction of all the parts. For Panikar the fundamental monastic principle is Blessed Simplicity. The monk is the one who learns to say 'no' to all that fragments or creates barriers. But the modern monk does not say 'no' to anything that is real; he achieves simplicity through integration, not denial. Panikar quotes John of the Cross:

> If you wish to enjoy all
> wish to possess nothing.
> If you wish to be all
> wish to be nothing

In his book *The Twilight of American Culture* social critic Morris Berman observes that we live 'in a collective adrenaline rush, a world of endless promotional/commercial bullshit that masks a deep systemic emptiness.'

He believes that if our civilisation is to be saved, only 'the new monastic individual' (NMI) will have the capacity to do so: someone who 'sees through his or her own cultural conditioning and refuses to be blindly driven any longer by the heroic program of power and achievement ... You can choose a way of life that becomes its own 'monastery', preserves the treasures of our heritage for yourself, and, hopefully, for future generations ... You and I can lead the monastic life and we can start to do it right now.'[53]

[53] See Berman, Morris (2000) *The Twilight of American Culture*, W. W. Norton & Co.

As I have reflected upon the writings of Panikar and others, and my own experiences, I have chrystallised 'Five marks of the Inner Monk'. These are:

1. Living for God alone

A young married Christian leader writes that during a pilgrimage the theme of his daily prayers has been 'nothing but God'; that is about being dependent on nothing but God. The stories of Elijah and the widow and Hagar and Ishmael have been very meaningful to me in recent times and I think it is because they had nothing left to depend on except God. A new monastic makes a contract with his soul friend to seek God alone, decides which distractions he will cut himself off from, and which commitments (e.g. marriage or work) he will honour as a means of honouring God.

2. Being who you are

Just being who you are
not justifying or apologising.
It sounds so easy
it's a life work
not to get caught in
producing
performing
proving
keeping accounts of indebtedness
waiting for gratitude
reward ambition
manipulation
staggering self-pity
but cultivating
the habit of being.[54]

[54] *The Habit of Being – Letters of Flannery O'Connor* (1979) Farrar, Straus & Giroux.

A true monk never takes a holiday from being a monk; that would indicate (s)he is fragmented. You are a monk twenty-four hours a day, seven days a week, all the days of the year whether on holiday or not.

3. Patient ripening

To let each impression and each germ of a feeling come to completion wholly in itself, in the dark, in the inexpressible, the unconscious, beyond the reach of one's own intelligence, and await with deep humility and patience the birth-hour of a new clarity . . . not reckoning and counting, but ripening like the tree which does not force its sap and stands confident in the storms of spring without the fear that after them may come no summer. It does come. But it comes only to the patient, who are there as though eternity lay before them, so unconcernedly still and wide.[55]

A monk is a person who always knows what they are supposed to do at a given time. Obedience is loving listening and a readiness to respond.

4. Spaces for solitude

For C. G. Jung noise was the degenerative symptom of urban civilisation. He concluded that as people's fear of nuclear tragedy, over-population or planetary pollution increased, their unconscious fear was reproduced, at a conscious level, as love of noise, which stops the fear being heard. Noise drowns the instinctive warnings of global catastrophe. It gives a false sense of security, it crowds out painful reflections. The real fear was what

[55] From Rilke, Rainer Maria and Herter Norton, M. D. (trs.) (1954) *Letters to a Young Poet*.

might come up from the depths if there was silence – all those things previously held at bay by noise. He also felt children's lack of concentration, about which Swiss educationalists were complaining, came about because all the important stimuli were external, for example radio and television.

A new monastic decides with his soul friend, and if necessary, with his family or colleagues, when and how to create regular zones of silence, and (s)he will also build in regular days or weeks of retreat. St Antony said:

> Just as a fish that stays too long on land will die, so monks who spend too long with the world are torn away from a disposition to silence. The rationale for monasticism could be most succinctly described as an effort to live in the now ... one way of achieving that is to follow the natural rhythm of the hours of the day.[56]

5. A heart of mercy towards all creation

When Abba Joseph asked an elder how he could become a monk, the elder told him he would be a monk when he never judged anyone. Abba Isaac was asked What is a merciful heart? His answer: 'A heart burning for the whole of creation, for people, birds, animals, demons and for every creature. Eyes running with tears at seeing and recalling all these.' To the monastic, Descartes' dictum 'I think therefore I am' pales into insignificance besides the monk's dictum: 'I forgive, therefore I am.'

---

[56] Steidl-Rast, David, (2001) *The Music of Silence: a sacred journey through the hours of the day*, Ulysses Press.

In his book *Finding the Monk Within: Great Monastic Values for Today*, Edward G. Sellner highlights the lives of ten monastic pioneers and their partners, from Antony of Egypt to Bernard of Clairvaux, and deduces these monastic values which he believes anyone today may make their own:

Sharing stories (Athanasius).

Silence, solitude and discernment (Antony and the desert monastics).

Faith in its communal dimension (Martin of Tours and Hilary of Poitiers).

Friendship and God's life revealed in our erotic side (Augustine and Monica).

Transparency with a spiritual mentor (Jerome and the desert mothers).

Compassion and the inclusion of lay monastics (Brigid and the Irish monastics).

Integrating contemplation with our daily life (Gregory the Great).

Stability and love (Benedict and Scholastica)

Learning to read 'the book of experience' (Bernard).[57]

Sellner concludes that these are not only monastic values, they are values of the soul – 'and they apply to everyone, regardless of gender, occupation, material status or place of residence.'

Thomas Merton, the Christian monk who studied Buddhist traditions equated the monastic journey with that of the journey each person needs to make away from ego, power and acquisitiveness towards 'the true self' which grows out of forgiveness, compassion, generosity and hospitality.

[57] Quoted in Sellner, Edward C. (2008) *Finding the Monk Within: Great Monastic Values for Today*, Hidden Spring, an imprint of Paulist Press.

An impractical ideal?

Is all this a romantic ideal that cannot be sustained outside ordered precincts? It seems that even the greatest of popes thought so. In AD 590 the monk Gregory was propelled into the papacy – the busiest job imaginable – at a time when Rome was besieged by political turmoil and the Church in many lands demanded his attention. In a homily on the book of Ezekiel he wrote:

> When I lived in a monastic community I was able to keep my tongue from idle topics and to devote my mind almost continually to the discipline of prayer. Since taking on my shoulders the burden of pastoral care, I have been unable to keep steadily recollected because my mind is distracted by many responsibilities. I am forced to consider questions affecting churches and monasteries ... at one moment I am forced to take part in certain civil affairs, next I must worry over the incursions of barbarians ... My mind is sundered and torn to pieces by the many and serious things I have to think about ... If I preserved the rigorously inflexible mode of speech that my conscience dictates, I know that the weaker sort of people would recoil from me and that I could never attract them to the goal I desire for them. So I must frequently listen patiently to their aimless chatter ... And yet the creator and redeemer of humankind can give me, unworthy though I be, the grace to see life whole and power to speak effectively of it.[58]

I empathise with Gregory for, in a much smaller way, I have a foot in both camps – the monastic and the marketplace.

---

[58] Brother Kenneth (ed), homilies of Pope Gregory I on Ezekiel quoted in *The Fathers to the Churches*, Collins (1985).

My hunch is that Gregory's greatness as pope was made possible and sustained by the mindset, disciplines and memories of his time as a monk. Postmodern monks may work in the turmoil of the marketplace, but they often repair to the monastery, the poustinia, or to the inner place of sanctuary. Their lives consist of a dialogue between these two worlds.

What can we learn from the Celtic Monastic Movement?

Andy Freeman of the 24/7 prayer movement have written extensively about what we can learn today from the Celtic monastic movement. The rest of this chapter consists of extracts from *Punk Monk*:

> Within the postmodern culture, there is a longing for 1) deeper community, 2) an experiential spirituality, and 3) an adventure. This is evidenced by disintegration of families and increased loneliness, the increasing interest in New Age, Eastern religion, and neopaganism, and the inception of adventure TV and game shows. How can the Western Church answer these cries when she doesn't even know how to answer them herself? Where can she go for answers? Many Christians are beginning to reopen the spiritual wells of history to find answers. Many believe that the renewal of interest in the Celtic Christian movement is part of the Holy Spirit's answer to prayers for revival. I will seek to demonstrate how digging up the ancient wells of Celtic Christianity and in particular, Celtic monasticism, can bring revelation to these three cries of postmodern culture.
>
> The foundation for the establishment of Celtic monasticism was obviously the conversion of the Celts.

Up to this point in Irish history, the Celts were known as fearless warriors. Their pagan priests known as druids would often offer their best men to angry, bloodthirsty gods who demanded human sacrifice. Thus, the Celts understood the true connotations of sacrifice, for it was written deep within their culture. This set the stage for the arrival of the Gospel. For it was in the realisation that the true God loved them rather than hated them that the Irish sacrificed their own lives (this time living, not dead sacrifices; Romans 12:1, 2) for the Gospel. These living martyrs realised that no sacrifice was too big in comparison to the ultimate sacrifice that God had made for them. Realising that Jesus had died for them created a sacrificial ethic within Irish believers. This warrior, sacrificial spirit would soon be infused into different types of martyrdom for Christ such as green and white. Thomas Cahill writes:

> 'The Green martyrs were those who, leaving behind the comforts and pleasures of ordinary human society, retreated to the woods, or to a mountaintop, or to a lonely island to one of the green noman's lands outside tribal jurisdictions, there to study the scriptures and commune with God.'[59]

However, this appeared to fail because each time a Green martyr left many would follow them and want to imitate their way of life. This resulted in the conception of Irish monasticism.

What did the structure of these Irish monasteries look like? Church leadership revolved around a community.

---

[59] Cahill, Thomas (1997) *How the Irish Saved Civilisation*, Bantam Doubleday.

People interacted with each other through daily life rather than just one day a week. Ministry took place daily and, 'Much of their work was probably done in the open air or in people's homes rather than in designated ecclesiastical buildings.'[60] An application of this kind of structure today could answer a lot of the deep cries for closer community in today's individualistic society and big mega-churches. There are already movements in the church today which mirror this, such as the house church and cell church movements, which seek to bring believers together into smaller more intimate fellowships. However, it is likely that for greater change to occur, it would require a complete revolution of church structure from being institutional to communal. Church leaders would shepherd small communities rather than large congregations. This structure would allow people to be more involved in each other's lives rather than distant. Indeed, this would require an ideological re-definition of what the word church means (not a place to meet, but a group of people who are the Church). This is happening today.

Other elements of Celtic communities that can prophesy to us today are their concepts of teams and leadership structure. For the Celts, ministry in all its aspects – liturgical, pastoral, evangelistic, educational, was not the solitary individualistic task it so often is today. It was rather undertaken by teams of men and women, ordained and lay, who lived together in community and operated from a common central base from which they went out among the people preaching, teaching, baptising, administering the sacraments, caring for the sick and burying the dead.

[60] Bradley, Ian (2000) *Colonies of Heaven: Celtic Models for Today's Church*, DLT.

The team implied a wide diversity of callings and vocations, each one being able to contribute to the whole. In our individualistic society it is easy to thrust one person into a church leadership role and expect that person to meet all the spiritual needs of the people. This is likely one main reason there is so much burnout amongst pastors today. Most evangelicals associate the word monk, and monastery, with celibacy, separation from the world and endless hours of fasting, chanting, and praying. This was not the complete picture in these Celtic monasteries. They were centres of culture and community. In fact, this was the primary difference between the Celtic monastic movement and its mother monastic movement derived from the Desert Fathers in Egypt. In stark contrast to the Desert Fathers who generally sought and practised radical separation from the world, many of the monasteries in the British Isles were intensely involved in the world and the lives of the people they served as well as being places of withdrawal and sanctuary. In scattered rural communities with virtually no other institutions or centres, they fulfilled the roles of hospital, hotel, school, university, arts workshop, open prison and reformatory, night shelter and drop-in day centre as well as church, retreat house, mission station and place of prayer and spiritual healing. They concerned themselves not just with spiritual, intellectual and physical well-being of the tribal communities which they served but also with their culture and tradition. As well as copying the psalms and gospels, those working in the monastic scriptoria wrote down for posterity the stories, poems and songs of pre-Christian Celtic culture.

Not all monasteries served all of these functions. As mentioned previously, they were highly diversified.

Some existed primarily as retreats and houses of prayer, others as bases for missionary work and pastoral care. The pastoral care within these monasteries was one of presence. This is to say that people in the tribal community would go to the monastery for pastoral care rather than have the monks come to them. The monasteries were known as places of healing. But above all else the Celtic monasteries were known as places of prayer. Prayer was at the centre of monastic life. It was the lungs that brought breaths of life to the community. The Celtic monks understood that nothing happens without prayer. Today, there is a renewal of prayer houses and retreats.

For these Celtic monks, White Martyrdom was the equivalent of true pilgrimage. (In contrast to Red martyrs who gave up their lives for Christ by embracing physical death, in the early Irish tradition White Martyrs gave up their lives by going into exile from their home comforts.) This definition of pilgrimage is a far cry from the twentieth-century definition today, which simply equates to travelling towards or on a sacred path for a spiritual high and then returning home. For these monks it literally meant abandoning house and homeland without the probability of return. What an adventure! This kind of adventure is becoming increasingly attractive because people are weary of a Christian spirituality that is structured, manufactured, and controlled. There is an increasing longing for a wild, indigenous, and Spirit-led Christianity. The application of this element of adventure, sojourning, or pilgrimage can be seen in various aspects of life. The Christian life is a journey that may take unexpected turns. Spontaneity and flexibility can teach us that it's OK to take a different turn in life whether it be minor or major. There seems to be a pressure within North American culture to have a two-, five-, or ten-year plan. What if the Holy Spirit communicates a change of plans or directions to us? Celtic spirituality encourages us to embrace these changes. In fact the possibility of change can even be exciting and all a part of the journey of the Christian.

Walking in daily spiritual experience or being aware of God's presence in everyday life, through the ordinary and the extraordinary was something that characterised the life of a Celtic Christian. As mentioned previously there is an increasing longing for this again today. Within the classical tradition that influences the North American church, the Holy Spirit is often restricted to speaking only through a minister preaching a sermon on a Sunday, or through our daily devotional reading. While this is crucial, the Celts can teach us that the Holy Spirit is not limited to these mediums of communication. This comes from a conviction that there is a thin wall separating the natural and the supernatural. Thus, both can speak to us. An animal, the wind, sunshine, or a body of water could reveal something about God or what he wants us to do. As well, there are many accounts of dreams, visions, and angelic visitations given to us by the Celts.

Within the postmodern culture, there is a longing for deeper community, an experiential spirituality, and an adventure. These three elements came alive for me as I traced the movement of Celtic monasticism. Is it possible that a new monasticism using elements of Celtic monasticism could be part of the Holy Spirit's answer to cries for renewal in the Western church? Furthermore, in addition to bringing renewal to the church could it also be part of the evangelistic answer to reaching a culture which longs for community, spiritual experience, and adventure?

CHAPTER 5

Monastic churches and villages of God

If there is an element of the monk in every human being, could there be an element of the monastery in every church? Until recently there would have been an emphatic 'no' to such a question, but statistics tell a remorseless story that may make us think again. In Europe church-going continues to decline steeply, while interest in spirituality continues to increase. The elements that postmodern people dislike in churches are the non-monastic elements: they don't want to be berated, they don't want a one-service-must-fit-all church, they don't want more words, packaged programmes, committees, talk-shops, pigeon-holing. Elements that sincere spiritual seekers desire may be found in monasticism: space for mysticism, spiritual formation and a path to follow, a place where they can come and go, eat or stay overnight and be themselves. 'Churches' of fast-growing non-Christian religions are more like monasteries than single congregations. The largest gurdwara outside India, which opened in Southall, near London, in 2003 is a seven-days-a-week place for eating, education, prayer and beauty.

The local church in Eastern Orthodoxy has never entirely lost the link with the monastery. Every bishop is a monk, and many worshippers will have some acquaintance with a monastery. Now, in Western churches which have long had no link with a monastery, experiments are taking place which could be said to incorporate one or other element of a monastic tradition. For example, a fresh expressions church creates a 'Sunday Morning Experience': anyone may come in and out to read newpapers, drink coffee, have conversations, try out prayer stations; drop in on children's activities, an adult act of worship, or sit in the garden.

Jesus called us to relate our work for God to the changing nature of the times (Luke 12:54–56). In my Forrester lecture *Does the Future Have a Church?* at Saint Andrews University in 2005 I argued as follows:

> The fact that in many parts of Europe the models of church that have withstood ravages of centuries are near the end of their shelf life is causing Christians in churches which have little in common theologically to relate to the changing context of society. What sort of things are they finding?
>
> - That in a twenty-four-hour society people relate better to seven-days-a-week churches.
>
> - That in a multi-choice society people look to churches that offer facilities for a range of temperaments, cultures and ages.
>
> - That in what the restauranteur Sir Terence Conrad calls the emerging café society, where people gather to do all sorts of things besides eat and drink, churches are eating places as well as praying places.
>
> - That in a visual, soundbite age people resort to churches that use different media – poetry as well as pulpits, storytelling as well as sermons.
>
> - That in an age of mass travel, when people look for B&Bs and hostels that they can relate to, churches provide accommodation – in their grounds, or on their websites. They once again link up with hostel and guest house movements.

- That in a multi-ethnic society people expect to find within the wider church services that are culturally Muslim or Sikh in style.

- That in an orphaned society, when mentors, life coaches and growth buddies are in demand in the worlds of business, fitness and AIDS care, people seek out spiritual homes where they can find soul friends and mentors.

- That in a packaged, pressured society suffering from data overload and stressful bureaucracy people make a beeline for churches where they can chill out, be themselves, have space.

- That in a world where equality of regard is written into statutes few people under forty any longer wish to be defined by a protest movement of 450 years ago called the Reformation, but are drawn to churches that are transcending the Protestant or Catholic label.

Existing churches are restoring certain monastic features. A growing number provide daily public prayer, cafés, conference facilities or work projects. Such churches are listed on the Community of Aidan and Hilda website www.aidanandhilda.org

Moreover, people in churches are having visions of their congregations being transformed into monasteries. A Canadian Vineyard leader, Peter Fitch, wrote in an article:

Last fall I had an opportunity to spend some time at the Cambridge Vineyard's new home, a Slovakian Jesuit monastery that lies hidden behind a park in the heart of the city. The grounds are beautiful and when I was there the buildings were in the process of being hastened back to life by an army of volunteers. I spent a quiet hour or two on the property one day and found myself reflecting about the irony of a new-styled church in an older-styled home. It fits so well with the cry for an ancient-future church that Robert Webber, Thomas Oden and others have been raising in their books and articles.[61]

It also fits with something very dear to my own heart. Over the past number of years I've been teaching a course called Ministry Skills and Issues in the Master of Ministry Program that I direct at St Stephen's University in St Stephen, New Brunswick. In the course, students read many ancient Christian works, and together we sit at a round table and discuss the relevance of the ideas to the churches that are forming today. I've become convinced that older writings contain substance, wisdom, beauty, and attitudes that we must not lose as we ramble through postmodernism and head for whatever comes next. As we stretch for the future we need to be grounded in the past.

Sitting in an office I looked out over the grounds and I rejoiced at the Lord's gift to this church. Suddenly I sensed that he was leading my reflections. Most people who have lived their lives in monasteries have taken a three-fold vow of poverty, chastity and obedience. Although I've appreciated the motivation behind the vows, I've always felt that monks missed an important part of being in the world, but none of it with this approach. I love a great deal of St Augustine's writing, for instance, but I've grown used to simply discarding anything that he has to say about family matters. From the time in the Confessions when he recorded his second

---

[61] The late Robert Webber wrote a series of Ancient-Future books such as *Ancient-Future Faith: Rethinking Evangelism in a Postmodern World*, Baker Books (1999) and *Ancient-Future Evangelism: Making Your Church a Faith-Forming Community*, Baker Books (2002).

most famous prayer, 'Lord, grant me chastity, but not yet!' he consistently sought or wrestled with the need for a full conversion, not just to Jesus but to celibacy. That this was, in his mind, a necessary part of any conversion worth having is, to my mind, a tragedy.

On the other hand, I have to agree with Richard Foster and others who have chastised the contemporary church for looking suspiciously like the rest of the world in regard to issues of money, sex and power. It's easy to believe that something is missing in this approach too.

Where is the proper path? What is it like? Gradually I felt the Lord pointing me to something that went beyond the mistakes of the past or the present. I'm not looking for poverty, he seemed to say, but for a prosperity of contentment, whether someone has a lot or a little, that issues forth in generosity. I'm not looking for chastity, but for a purity of spirit and body, whether a person is single or married, that allows him or her to be devoted to my purposes and yielded to my ways. (I immediately sensed that for most of us this would include a level of sexual healing, and that the Lord knew this very well and was at peace with the idea. I also sensed that he was willing to offer it.) Finally, I heard this idea: I'm not looking for unswerving obedience to a spiritual director or to a person or to an institution, or even to a way of doing things; rather, I desire a mutuality of submission in leaders and followers that allows them to bend towards the needs and cares that they find in each other and produces the kind of unity that pushes back darkness and shows the world something of my character.

At the end of the reflection I was seeing a form of spiritual monastery rising up in cities and towns all over our land. It was connected to the passion and faithfulness that led ancient Christians to make so many sacrifices, but it was also full of serious engagement with the world as it now is. The city of God was being planted, not in a desert, or on a hill, but right in the midst of the city of man. The spiritual buildings seemed defined by balloons of joy that were leaving the hands of people on the ground and reaching for heaven. Every living church got to play its part, and all of the people, men and women and children, lived on holy ground as they kept thankful and obedient hearts in the midst of the various communities in which they lived. Their prayers, at times ordered and at times spontaneous, were like the Benedictine hours of the Divine Office. Their songs, whether gentle or wild, whether acoustic, electric, or digital, echoed the meaning of Gregorian chants. Their healing compassion for the broken ones around them was like the Franciscan care of lepers. Their devotion to the word of God or to the teaching ministry of the Church was reminiscent of the Dominicans or the Jesuits as they travelled to spread the Gospel far and wide. And their growing intimacy with God was a picture of the Cistercians, particularly of Bernard of Clairvaux who preached 86 rapturous sermons on the Song of Songs, only to make it to Chapter 2, verse 1!

When I think of it now, I like to reflect on one additional aspect of a new monasticism: the cultivation of silence that in the end produces a powerful word from God. Long before the Trappists, ancient Christians suspected that this was the truth. Ignatius of Antioch, who was martyred around AD 107, wrote this to the Ephesian church:

A man who has truly mastered the utterances of Jesus will also be able to apprehend his silence, and thus reach full spiritual maturity, so that his own words have the force of actions and his silences the significance of speech...

The Cambridge Vineyard, with its strong but humble leaders, its wonderful worship music, its determined focus upon children and mercy ministries, as well as its emphasis upon camaraderie and fellowship, became for me a prophetic picture of God's longing for a new monasticism in the twenty-first century. Not all of our churches will acquire monasteries or traditional church buildings. However, all can become strong and beautiful communities of faith and action that rise up and fill the land with the best intentions of the past and their appropriate fulfilments in the present and the future. May it be so! (www.scvine.com)

The Monastery of the Transfiguration

Visions like that of Peter Fitch increase, but does anyone actually make them happen? The Monastery of the Transfiguration has been a centre of renewal in Breakwater, Geelong, Australia. The community is unique in that it continued the life and witness of a 135-year old Baptist congregation while drawing on classic sources of monasticism. It began in the early 1970s. Graeme Littleton and Steven Shipman studied the Rule of Benedict, Orthodox sources, and a number of models of communal life, including Ephrata, an Anabaptist experiment that began in the eighteenth century in Lancaster County, Pennsylvania. As the community grew, members developed a Resolve, the practices by which they live, which include: Love God, neighbour, all creation; judge no one, not even yourself; love beauty; maintain inner silence; show hospitality, err only on the side of generosity; speak truth to power, especially power without love; let your only experience of evil be in suffering, not its creation.

The community has over 30 members who until recently lived in the Cloister or nearby. Members observe traditional monastic commitments to hospitality, obedience, stability, and a balanced life of prayer and work. While several members have chosen a celibate life, married couples also live in the Cloister. Families live in houses, while the celibate sisters and brothers live in single-sex households. Members support themselves through ordinary work. In accord with Acts 2:45 and Acts 4:34, 12 live under the common purse, while members of the Greater Community tithe. A communal meal shared by many visitors follows the Eucharist. The Monastery has attracted to its membership several master crafts persons and artists. The icons, vestments, architecture, stained glass, and other artistic features embody monastic values of simplicity and holiness. Members seek to respect the beauty of creation. With three buildings set aside for worship specifically, nearly a dozen houses, gardens, and a guest house, the property encompassed two acres. Once a garbage heap, the Cloister became a protected bird sanctuary. The community attracts members from many denominations, including the Anglican, Baptist, Catholic, and Uniting churches of Australia.

In 2008 the community made the brave decision to relocate to a large Greenfield site where they are planning a purpose-built monastic settlement that will cater for their growing numbers. And once again, they will be the church for their area.[62]

Urban Seed

During my recent travels in Australia I led a day workshop on the new monasticism in Melbourne. No less than five small groups present at that one meeting had begun a new monastic experiment. Three ladies described their community as 'a

---

[62] Dekar, Paul R. (2008) *Community of the Transfiguration: The Journey of a New Monastic Community*, Cascade Books New Monastic Library.

cathedral without walls'. My host, Brent Lyons Lee, works for Urban Seed, a social project, but has been seconded to be minister of Norlane Baptist Church for two days a week. This church, in a needy suburb of Geelong, was near to closure. The Baptist Union of Victoria State agreed that Urban Seed could build accommodation units, create a refectory that provides free meals to the unemployed, and a sacred space that is always open. Brent nicknames the re-formed church 'the seedy monastery'. Brent and his family hope to buy a house next to the church, turn its large plot into a community garden, and commence daily corporate prayer. He writes:

> Because we don't constitutionally exist as a church with the Baptist Union, we have come under the 'new missional community' banner with the Baptist Union of Victoria. This is a learning experience for the denomination as well as the new communities that are coming into being.[63]

I visited Bendigo, a gold rush town. There several young Urban Seed people have bought houses near to each other, to form a community of daily prayer and outreach. They are negotiating with a little-used Anglican church as to whether this could become their base.

Faith Community in Earls Court, London

In London a young man named Tom Gillum was inspired by his visit to the Community of Sant'Egidio in Rome. Some well-educated young Romans wanted to live out their faith and connect with the poor. In 2004 the Bishop of Kensington, London, who had observed how Tom had established a faith community in a redundant church building with 35 others from Holy Trinity Church, Brompton, invited him with his wife and

[63] Lyons Lee, Brent & Simpson, Ray (2008) *Emerging Down Under*, ATF Press.

five children, to move into St Jude's Vicarage at Earls Court and establish a fresh expression of church – a non-parochial, small, quality community of people committed to live with the poor and to pray. They meet for daily prayer together, including Night Prayer on Tuesdays and Fridays. Currently jazz musician David Okumu is helping them to see in jazz a unique way of affirming community.[64]

Can congregations become monasteries?

Monasteries can be churches, and redundant churches can house a new community, but at first sight it seems unlikely that congregations can become monasteries. One reason is that leaders of churches are appointed by bishops or boards with a non-monastic agenda. In religious communities, in contrast, the spiritual leader evolves from within in an organic relationship of unconditional commitment. A second reason is that in monasteries the core members commit to be available for certain duties and to live by values for which they are held accountable. Church members are not required to make such commitments. A third reason is that churches employ staff with pay differentials; in monasteries everyone is equal. Although it seems unlikely that churches can become monasteries, church commissions and reports press for radical change from the one-service-only congregation.

I am gripped, therefore, by an initiative of Simon Reed, a colleague in the Community of Aidan and Hilda, who has written the appendix to this book. He is Vicar of a small Anglican church on the edge of an estate of commuters, beside a busy, uncrossable circular road. The site lacks any of the features one associates with a monastic church. Yet Simon has articulated to his congregation the three things he believes are essential for a monastic church: members who commit to a Way of Life, a rhythm of prayer and a network of soul friends. The congregation is currently exploring these three things. If they embrace them, it will, I believe, mark a significant moment in 'ordinary' church life in Britain.

Non-parochial expressions of Church

The Church of England's 2004 report *Mission-Shaped Church* calls for radical new forms of church. The monastic church, however, is not mission driven, it is God driven. By modelling the life of God, mission through magnetism takes place.

Some Anglican/Episcopal Dioceses now permit non-parochial expressions of church to be established and these may be faith communities served by a dispersed community. Jerry Doherty, an Episcopalian priest in the USA introduced a Rule when he was rector of the Church of the Ascension in Stillwater, Minnesota. He has launched The Caim which embraces those who follow this Rule. The Caim is the name of his Order or networking. The word 'caim' is Irish for 'circling'. He says that whereas most declining churches try out ideas from the business world, and leave the spiritual world untapped, the monastic thing begins in a church that is open to try something more meaningful. For example, a church in a city centre combines a soup kitchen with daily prayer.

Willow Creek, USA

An example of a widely influential church that has recognised that its previous (decidedly unmonastic) approach needs to be unlearned is Willow Creek, USA, which has put vast sums of money into its programmes. Recently its leader, Bill Hybels, to his great credit confessed that they had got things wrong. His vision had been heavily influenced by the methods of secular business. James Twitchell, in his new book *Shopping for*

God,[65] reports that outside Bill Hybels' office hangs a poster that says: 'What is our business? Who is our customer? What does the customer consider value?' Directly or indirectly, this philosophy of ministry – church should be a big box with programmes for people at every level of spiritual maturity to consume and engage – has impacted almost every evangelical church in the country. However, recently Willow Creek released its findings from a multiple year qualitative study of its ministry. Basically, they wanted to know what programmes and activities of the church were actually helping people mature spiritually and which were not. The results were published in a book, *Reveal: Where Are You?*, co-authored by Greg Hawkins, executive pastor of Willow Creek[66] Having put so many of their eggs into the programme-driven church basket, you can understand their shock when the research revealed that:

> Increasing levels of participation in these sets of activities does *not* predict whether someone's becoming more of a disciple of Christ. It does *not* predict whether they love God more or they love people more.

Having spent 30 years creating and promoting a multi-million-dollar organisation driven by programmes and measuring participation, and convincing other church leaders to do the same, you can see why Hybels called this research 'the wake-up call' of his adult life. Hybels confesses:

> We made a mistake. What we should have done when people crossed the line of faith and became Christians, we should have started telling people and teaching people that they have to take responsibility to become

[65] Twitchell, James, (2007) *Shopping for God: How Christianity went from in your heart to in your face,* Simon & Schuster.

[66] Hawkins, Greg & Parkinson, Cathy (2007), *Reveal: Where you are?* Willow Creek Association.

'self-feeders'. We should have gotten people, taught people, how to read their Bible between service, how to do the spiritual practices much more aggressively on their own.'

In other words, spiritual growth doesn't happen best by becoming dependent on elaborate church programmes but through the age-old spiritual practices of prayer, Bible reading, and relationships. And, ironically, these basic disciplines do not require multi-million dollar facilities and hundreds of staff to manage. Does this mark the end of Willow's 30 years of influence over the American church? Not according to Hawkins: Our dream is that we fundamentally change the way we do church. That we take out a clean sheet of paper and we rethink all of our old assumptions. Replace it with new insights.[67]

The Seekers Church, Washington

Monastic churches teach people a path, not a programme. Some churches are making the membership process synonymous with spiritual formation. The Church of the Saviour, Washington DC, has famously done this. Now, new churches are following its example.[68]

In 1985 the Revd David McKeithen came to Rockbridge United Methodist Church, which had voted to disband due to declining numbers in a changing neighbourhood. He drew new members who in effect planted a new church in the same building. Drawing much of their inspiration from the Church of the Saviour, Washington DC,[69] they committed themselves to a common life. Each member chooses a mission group, which meets one night a week for spiritual formation and another night for service in the neighbourhood. Each mission group

---

[67] See www.crosswalk.com/pastors/11558438.
[68] See www.seekerschurch.org
[69] See www.cofs.org

engages in a lengthy process of discerning a corporate call. One of them founded one of the first Christian cohousing communities in the USA, out of a desire to offer an indigenous presence.

The Seekers Church in Washington is led by some 20 Stewards who, over two years, take courses in a lay 'seminary', working with a sponsor to clarify individual spiritual practices; writing a spiritual autobiography, and raising financial support to at least 10 per cent of income. They too are an offspring of the Church of the Saviour. This ecumenical Christian church was founded in 1947 by Gordon Cosby and requires every member to be in spiritual formation and in a mission group. Rather than grow larger and more centralised, Gordon's vision was to stay small and poor, so in 1976, six little churches formed around housing (Jubilee), children (Seekers), hospitality (Potters House), polyculturalism (8th Day), public policy (Dunamis) and retreat (Dayspring). Each little church developed a distinctive style of worship, preparation for membership and mission. The level of commitment to the inward/outward journey is still a common thread.

Churches where people live on site

Burngreave Ashram

Sometimes a group of churches combine to establish a community. In 2001 Sheffield Inner City Ecumenical Mission launched the Burngreave Ashram in Spital Hill, a needy area of Sheffield with ethnic groups speaking 47 languages. The Ashram consists of three flats (in which members live), a vegetarian and fair trade shop run by volunteers, a complex of buildings used by community groups for rehabilitation, mental health art, children's art and drama, music-making and a weekly midday meditation, a centre for spirituality,

Bible study groups, inter-faith and justice work. It provides temporary accommodation for asylum seekers. Experiments such as this lack, however, the Rule of Life and daily prayer which are surely essential marks of anything that may be called monastic.[70]

Churches that are eating places

Trevor White, a guru of good restaurants, suggested on a BBC 4 radio programme (1 June 2008) that good restaurants are beyond price. We go there to relax with friends we enjoy, in an atmosphere that takes us away from the strains of the working week. A good restaurateur, he suggests, is a servant, a friend and a mid-wife. The old monasticism offered sparing fare in a sparse environment, but we could often relax there with friends. Some years ago we began a list on our web site of churches that have, or are, cafés. There are now too many to be on the list. Few of these cafés are open all week, or would get into the Egon Ronay Guide, and some are staffed by employees who do not live the ethos or the Rule of the church, but this is a hopeful trend. Could one expression of the new monasticism be to offer 'down town' cafés, with vouchers for those unable to pay, and another expression be restaurants that offer good food in a good atmosphere, that are commercially run, but staffed by those who live the monastic ethos?

City Monastic Network Churches

Balham Community Church

Balham Community Church (BCC), South London, has explored the concept of a non-residential (i.e. network) monastery church within the following four circles:

[70] See www.ashram.org.uk

1. The Core

   This consists of those who live the BCC Values and carry out its work most days of the week.

2. The Congregation

   This consists of the wider number for whom BCC is their primary focus for worship, discipleship and enabling for their service in the wider world.

3. The Friends

   This consists of those in the wider community who relate to BCC for certain purposes but who make no primary commitment to it. It includes those who: join in activities, cells, training courses, special worship services; seek personal guidance from pastors, mentors, members; request rites of passage; enjoy friendship or common interests with BCC members.

4. The Wider World

   BCC may interact with the wider world by building relationships with local, city or national leaders, agencies and media; standing up for justice for oppressed individuals or groups; taking actions to improve the environment.

   Perhaps others can put flesh to this concept.

Emerging villages of God

Second, millennium monasteries were removed from the market-place, unsuited to people in the street, and gave little scope for varied and unfolding expressions of the Rule. Although new monasticism addresses these issues, it is a kaleidoscope of separate groups on the margins of society. Attempts to turn congregations into 'new monasteries' have barely begun and in the main seem unattainable.

Yet the world cries out for an accessible alternative to greed-fuelled capitalism. Increasing numbers of people aspire to be holistic. If these isolated monastic groups can join up with holistic expressions of work, commerce, culture, education and spirituality they could model what people aspire to. They could move from the edge to the hub.

It has happened before. As we have seen, the early Celtic monasteries were the hubs of their tribe. Our society is not tribal in the same sense (although ethnic minorities increase) but, because it is fluid, people can coalesce around shopping, leisure, cultural activities, work and education centres in village or city, and around 'virtual' internet hubs.

In my book *Church of the Isles: the emerging Church in Britain and Ireland – a prophetic strategy for renewal,*[71] I argued that nothing less than 'villages of God' could make possible what is needed to meet the spiritual need of our changing society.

This proposal proved too radical for many, and indeed, strays from my own preferred methodology of journeying with churches, as well as individuals, from the place where they are.

Yet, this back-to-the-future idea has been attempted to a degree even last century. In the 1920s Father Basil Jellicoe declared a 'war on slums' in Somers Town, London. He established the pioneering St Pancras House Improvement Society to prove that even the worst housing could be replaced and even the poorest tenants could have decent surroundings. He established nursery schools, community centres and works of art to decorate the courtyards and gardens. The sculptor Gilbert Bayes was commissioned to create ceramic finials to top the washing line posts in several courtyards. His main sources of inspiration were folklore, the Bible and medieval

[71] Simpson, Ray, (2003) *Church of the Isles: the emerging Church in Britain and Ireland – a prophetic strategy for renewal,* Kevin Mayhew Publishers.

romances. Many of his finials symbolised episodes in the lives of saints.

Villages of God take into account that traditional forms of church are coming to the end of their shelf-life.

They take into account that at the same time that there is a decline in the 'one-shape-fits-all' type of church, which post-modern people link with the power games of history – Protestant and Papist – there is a rising thirst for spirituality, values and gathering places that sustain life together on earth.

In the UK new structures are emerging following political devolution and economic and environmental cross-border partnerships. These new structures need undergirding through freshly evolving institutions, technology and places of spirituality.

The mushrooming of Christian projects, culture-friendly church plants and networks alongside the decline in the 'one-shape-fits-all' type of church makes possible patterns that are more flexible than the old. In the spirit of Jeremiah who called God's people to seek the good of the city (Jeremiah 29:7) some Christians have the vision of patterns emerging that cohere around some common values, facilities and rhythms. Certain of these 'villages' will be in one geographical area, others will be more dispersed but their various parts are linked by pilgrim trails and websites, and some may be virtual.

Clearing up misconceptions

Before I introduce the features of a village of God I will clear up some misconceptions. No one village of God will have all the features. Only a few can have most of these features on one site. Small churches, monastic households and projects in an area can use the village of God as a concept: by imaginatively linking new networks with traditional churches the margin-alised parts can become part of a greater whole, identify and use their resources to greater effect, and even link up with each other through pilgrim trails. Even an isolated church, although it cannot on its own be a village of God, can use the concept to appraise what features of a village it can offer – the most important being daily prayer and core values (basic values shared by all). Churches and groups in an area that at present are not connected can develop a virtual village of God through a shared website, inviting the public into their sacred and social spaces, their learning and leisure spaces, their creative and eco activities, their music and mentoring ministries.[72]

Villages of God start where people are. Some can grow piecemeal, others have a macro plan. A plan is not the return of the Christendom model – a model of Christianity which assumes that the Church's framework is the framework that the rest of society should accept and fit into.

These villages of God serve, they do not oust, the institutions that exist in their area – but like yeast in dough they inspire in them values such as trust, spirituality and service.

[72] One example is www.networkleeds.com

Members connect with supermarkets, nightclubs, schools, colleges and organisations.

Members connect with housing estates, pubs, organisations, networks, police, public services, media, homeless, prisons and gangs.

Members connect with town, health, community, leisure and education centres.

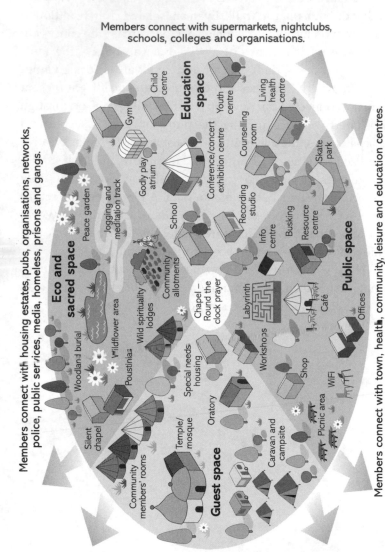

Education space
Child centre
Gym
Youth centre
Living health centre
Godly play atrium
Conference/concert exhibition centre
Counselling room
Recording studio
Skate park
School
Info centre
Busking
Resource centre

Public space
Labyrinth
Café
Offices

Eco and sacred space
Peace garden
Jogging and meditation track
Community allotments
Wild spirituality lodges
Wildflower area
Woodland burial
Poustinia

Chapel – Round the clock prayer

Workshops
Shop
WiFi
Special needs housing
Oratory

Guest space
Silent chapel
Community members' rooms
Temple/mosque
Caravan and campsite
Picnic area

Members connect with business, sports, internet, culture, churches and other faith communities.

Why the term 'village'?

In large cities, shopping centres and airports throughout the world you now see signs such as 'the village', 'youth city', 'waterside village', 'sky city', 'mediterranean village'. Even the Olympic Games now has a 'sports village'. Why? Because the marketeers know that people want something more than the sale of products – they want a feeling that they can be at home and in community. Of course, this is mostly a sham. Perhaps this will give 'village' such a bad name that the next generation will have to invent a new name. But for now it will do.

At the Church of Scotland's *Churches Without Walls 2008* gathering at Ingoldesthorpe near Edinburgh, a tent village was erected where representatives of two hundred churches told how God was leading them. This, too, indicates an aspiration.

What does a village of God offer?

It will offer some or all of these 'spaces'. The term 'space' may refer to a geographical area in the village that is set aside for a dedicated purpose, or to a metaphysical space, as in 'space in the programme'. These are the spaces:

The Core

This is a community who live by shared values or a Rule in or near the village.

Sacred Space

A rhythm of prayer once, twice or more each day. A silent area and praying places of different styles. A bell is rung at the hours of public prayer. The following words have been quoted from one of Henri Nouwen's books or broadcasts:

> I am deeply convinced that great renewal will develop wherever communities enter regularly into solitude.

Time for silence, individual study, personal prayer and meditation must be seen to be important to all the members of the community as working together, playing together and worshipping together. Without solitude we cannot experience each other as different manifestations of a love that transcends us all.

Eating space

A café, refectory or inn used by anyone in the village, and maybe also the public, ideally staffed by people who live the ethos of the village. In poorer areas soup kitchens and free meals may sometimes be offered free of charge.

Sleeping space

Accommodation units can take many forms: a hostel, en suite rooms, bed and breakfast offered by members of the village. The village may enter a partnership with a housing association to develop housing for people with special needs. It may have a retreat house, or small poustinias[73] in the secluded area to which individuals may come for a day, weeks or years of solitude. A village in a holiday area might include a caravan or campsite. If members of the core community or their friends have houses in or near the village they may provide a guest room in each house.

Eco-space

This may include a community allotment, a peace garden, poultry, a wild-flower area, bird sanctuary, park and picnic area. The village may develop partnerships with organisations such

[73] Poustinia is a Russian word meaning wilderness. In the West it refers to a simple room or building, with little else other than a cross, chair, table and perhaps provision for food and sleep. It is a place where an individual may spend time alone with God.

as Common Ground,[74] which aims to link nature with culture, and inspire action to improve the quality of everyday places. Gardens in a retreat area may include raised flower beds for people in wheelchairs and scented beds for the visually impaired.

An ideal village of God has a link to sustainable land, either on site or through a landholding elsewhere. Groups such as the Small Woods Association[75] provides help and information covering all aspects of woodland management and aims to restore the links between communities and local woodlands such as a woodland burial ground, a picnic area or a sponsor-a-tree programme.

The establishment of earth embassies in capital cities could be linked to a village of God. The mission of this movement is 'to inspire and educate the citizens of Earth to create their own environmentally sustainable lifestyles and businesses, through the creation of a self-sufficient education centre, organic farm, restaurant, fair-trade shop and eco-technology development demonstration centre. The Self-Sufficient Goals are to grow all our own fruit, vegetables etc., to collect and use only rain water, to recycle all our own waste, to produce our own energy, to educate the world.' (www.earthembassy.org)

I am told that Christ Church Anglican Cathedral, Ottawa, is exploring the possibility of its 'spare' land housing an Earth Embassy. This is the kind of development that villages of God in capital cities need to purse.

---

[74] Gold Hill House, 21 High Street, Shaftesbury, Dorset SP7 8JE 01747 850 820
HYPERLINK "http://www.commonground.org.uk"
[75] The Old Bakery, Pontesbury, Shropshire SY5 0RR 01743 792 644
HYPERLINK "http://www.smallwoods.org.uk"

Learning space

There may be a school and a child centre, life skills, discipling, fitness and meditation courses, an adult Sunday school, a computer room and library where students may study on their way home from school or work, and a resources centre. The village might sponsor lectures, dialogues and summer school. People are having new thoughts about the value of a Christian university. It is increasingly recognised that something was lost when the universities were removed from the monasteries. A Christian university can offer what John Henry Newman called 'universal knowledge' in which different parts of knowledge would be seen as parts of a whole, theology would be held in proper respect as 'the queen of sciences', the spiritual dimension of life would be integrated rather than marginalised, the study of the great world faiths would have an honoured place, specialisms would not push out study of the interrelations between disciplines, and students would have an experience of community which Christian values. make possible. Nowadays the energies of a secular university 'can all too easily be directed by political influences towards wealth creation and utilitarianism'.[76] Has not the time come for at least one 'high street monastery', backed by the churches, to establish a Christian university?

Play space

Sports facilities, a gym, a cyber café, a jogging/meditation trail, body-soul arts, e.g.Pilates, secure cycle racks, skate board facility.

Arts space

Exhibitions for local artists and photographers; a recording and practice music studio, creativity days, flower arranging, banner making, painting. Venue for gigs, concerts, storytelling.

[76] *Do We Need a Christian University?* Cambridge Papers volume 17 number 3, September 2008 by Nigel Paterson (The Jubilee Centre, Cambridge).

Multi-cultural celebration space

Parties, picnics, meetings, anniversaries, festivals. Tribe spaces (facilities for varied ages, cultures and temperaments).

'In my Father's house are many rooms' (John 14). In a colony of heaven there are provisions that suit many different types of people. Although the integrity of the Christian community must be guarded, there is no reason why, if there is a mosque, synagogue or temple in the area of the village, there could not be common eating and meeting places. Places such as St Catherine's monastery, Mount Sinai, have included a mosque since the first millennium.

Some church services are unsuited to young people. They don't want to sit in rows and be talked at. A worship experience which includes conversation, activity, eating and choice of prayer styles in a place with culture-friendly décor where they can hang out through the week will attract them. The same principle applies to some ethnic minorities. A village of God in a multi-cultural area should have a carpeted, oriental style building and an entrance where worshippers take off their shoes. It may have a Roman Catholic oratory with Exposition of the Blessed Sacrament, or a Quaker meeting room.

Children's space

The UK Government recently launched an initiative to help localities establish child centres. These not only include crèches, and pre-school groups, they involve parents and relatives in nurture and skill training, and in doing things together. In a village of God playing and praying, storytelling, learning-to read activities and godly play go hand in hand. There may be a children's play area, a soundproof, see-through crèche room, a nappy-changing room, and a godly play atrium.

Economic and work space

In the old monasteries work and prayer were inseparable, and so should they be, in a different way, in modern villages of God. A village may build workshops for use by members or for lease to others who share something of its values. It may have shops for faith resources, fair trade and local produce. It may invite companies to locate to the village site, or use the village for staff training and refreshment. It may run a credit union or a bread cooperative.

Multinational companies now recognise that the spiritual needs of the workforce need to be addressed if it is to be productive. They send staff for in-service training at places such as Douai Abbey near Reading in the UK. The Spirituality in the Workplace Network was set up in 2000 by Father Dermot Tredget, a Benedictine monk at Douai. They have a link with the US Management network Spirit in Work whose mission is to support global transformation by integrating spirituality and the workplace.[77] Businesses have become more powerful than governments. Since the scandals of the 2008 Great Credit Crunch the wrongness of focusing only on the bottom line (profit for those at the top) rather than on planetary sustainability and corporate well-being has become more apparent. People want the workplace to be a meaningful environment, as they spend on average more than 50 per cent of their time there. It is now more widely recognised that a combination of spiritual, emotional and intellectual intelligence enables the leader to achieve the organisation's goals in a more holistic manner, while at the same time meeting the needs of employees and the communities in which it operates. Spiritual leadership fosters a responsible relationship with the locality in which the workforce is based.[78] A village of God might even have

[77] See www.spiritatwork.org
[78] Danah Zohar & Ian Marshal write mass-market books on spiritual intelligence such as *Spiritual Intelligence*, Bloomsbury Paperbacks (2001).

a hotel if it is anything like *The Bio Seehotel Zeulenroda* – a leading conference hotel in Germany with a philosophy to value all living creatures and to live in harmony with everything.

Meeting space

The village has venues suitable for groups, conferences and interfaith dialogue. In a good village it will be possible to invite young people and ethnic minorities from areas of riot to meet people of their own age who treat them as special. Joseph Wakin, founder of the Australian Arabic Council said this after the riots in 2005 between Lebanese immigrants and older established Australians: 'the refrain of such folk is "on the streets I am king, everywhere else I am nothing." '[79] In a village of God they can be royal.

Public space

Villages of God that have a boundary with a busy throughway can provide a Wi-Fi area, a labyrinth, a drinking fountain, seats and picnic area as well as making public other parts of the village. Public premises can be hired by any groups who benefit the common good, and the village may itself host events for people in different walks of life such as interfaith dialogue. Musicians will busk in public spaces inside or outside the village. It may offer an Information Centre.

Motorway stop?

Might there be one village of God that encompasses a motorway stop? In England there is only one motorway stop that is locally owned and which has local character. This is the mission statement of Tebay Services, Westmorland, on the M6 between junctions 38 and 39:

> We are a small family business, home-grown, down-to-earth farmers, in love with Cumbria, protective of our

[79] Quoted from *The Age*, 14 December 2005.

environment, keen to promote local talent, proud of our homemade food, passionate about quality, honest, approachable, individual, loyal to our customers, always striving to be the very best in everything we undertake.

Westmorland Ltd. Welcome to our family village shop, farm shop – excellent home-bred lamb and beef from our farm; gift shop, coffee shop, outside BBQ, café, caravan park, excellent washrooms, picnic area, coffee shop, petrol, diesel and LPG, architecture that enhances lovely views.[80]

I make a point of stopping at this potential village of good: if it embraced sacred space, core community and prayer it could become a village of God.

The spokes of the village of God

The village of God is like a wheel with spokes that reach into the heart of society. The spokes take the form of being a supportive presence within the cultural patterns 'out there'. These may include:

- School
- College
- Health centre
- Supermarket
- Pub
- Sports teams
- Fitness centre
- Community centre
- Bingo club
- Uniformed organisations
- Police

[80] See www.westmorland.com

- Social services
- Local media
- Centres of other religions
- Places where disaffected groups hang out
- Night clubs
- The homeless
- Sink housing estates
- City centres at night
- Business houses
- Local government.

The values of a village of God

The values of some Christian missionary projects have driven away 'the tribes', who thought their identity would not be respected, and that they would feel invaded and violated. In order for a village that welcomes diversity to exist, a theology that undergirds this is essential. Villages of God presuppose certain common values without which they would fall apart. These values are likely to include: Respect for life, seeing Christ in the face of the other, and trust. Churches in villages of God acknowledge that the part is not the whole.

Values also include simplicity that sheds possessiveness; mercy that understands and does not condemn; hospitality that allows the other person and group to be themselves in our presence.

Eddie Gibbs and Ryan K. Bolger list what they think are essential values of the emergent church in their book.[81] They include the values of authenticity and openness. They omit other values without which the church cannot be sustained at the heart of modern life. For example, the rhythm of prayer and work, the creation of spaces, the reconnection with roots in

[81] *Emerging Churches: creating Christian community in postmodern cultures*, SPCK (2006).

the soil of sanctity and the soil of earth. An emergent church that has the values of the village of God:

- Worships God
- Listens and learns
- Celebrates creativity
- Sells ethical products
- Shares its goods
- Tends the earth
- Respects the styles of its peoples.

Planting people-friendly monastic communities that are born out of such a dynamic, and which do not have to be squeezed into a 'one-shape-fits-all' church structure, may be the only way to win our emerging society. For monasteries, whether old or new, are usually freed from 'normal' church regulations so that they can develop under God according to their own prophetic charisms (some people have gifts of seeing or of prophecy).

The villages enable churches to be true to themselves and be more sustaining of their society. In villages of God the prayer oratory of one tradition or the soup kitchen of another can be true to its root – but each can flower because it is in an environment that does not attack it. Villages of God become prejudice-free, hate-free, fear-free, earth-friendly fair trade zones. These villages of God offer the soil of reflection and the wisdom of the forgiving heart to which politicians and public may repair. They foster that love which inspires inner transformation, stable relationships, and motivation to live healthy, law-abiding, earth-cherishing lives.

Where do we look for villages of God?

Most villages of God grow naturally, like a mustard seed, and take a different form in each place. One may be sponsored by a large single church which develops seven-day-a-week facilities and links up with other networks. In some areas, the local church leaders forge a deep and prayerful relationship which transforms localities, as did relationships described in the DVD series *Transformations.*[82]

In the USA megachurches have some outward characteristics of the monastic village. They are places where members can not only pray, but work out in a gym, eat at a food court or browse in a bookstore. Prestonwood Baptist Church, Texas, is a sprawling campus of 140 acres. The Ellis family virtually lives there: 'Dad works out at Prestonwood, and Mom, Beth, teaches religion. The kids, Graham and Sheridan, hang out in the children's section, and their older sister, Landen, goes to school at Prestonwood and sings in the choir.' Prestonwood has sports fields, an arcade, small Bible-study groups and a bookstore on what is called Main Street. There is even a food court where the Ellises frequently eat, complete with a Starbucks coffee shop. Every weekend, there are three services to accommodate Prestonwood's membership of 24,000 people. 'It's like a small town in a big city,' said Beth Ellis.

Keith Meyer and his team at the 3000-member Church of the Open Door in Maple Grove, Minnesota, have asked questions such as 'Is megachurch discipleship an oxymoron?' and 'Must large mean shallow?'. They are committed to nurturing a core of disciples and they are looking for guidance to . . . the monastery. See the article 'The Megachurch and the Monastery' in *Leadership Weekly*, 3 March 2009.

Yet, generally speaking, megachurches are short-lived, like products that have a limited shelf-life rather than organisms that have a self-sustaining life. They are not born and bathed in prayer, purity and poverty of spirit. They are not monastic. They are not, by our definition, villages of God.

My visit to reviving Russian monasteries took me to Pskov. Here the monastery kremlin, with its monks, manual workers,

---

[82] See www.gatewaymedia.org.uk to obtain the DVD series

iconography school and refectory is at the heart of the small town, and its walls in no way isolate it from the shopping streets outside. I remember, for example, a stunning icon of Jesus with the woman at the Samaritan well in a prime position in the main street.

Pilgrim centres accrue elements of the village of God, specially islands such as Iona and Lindisfarne. These have sacred space and nature space, eating space and sleeping space, learning space and shop space. Because no one owns these different elements, there is truly unity in diversity. Pilgrims who visit the Holy Island of Lindisfarne, where I live, will find twice-daily prayer at St Mary's parish church. They can find places to sleep at retreat houses, self-catering cottages and hotels. St Mary's Franciscan Vicar Brother Damian, has a vocation to give up his own bed, if the vicarage is full of guests, and to sleep on the floor. The former Presbyterian Church, St Cuthbert's, which is now a Visitors'Centre, has turned its former vestry into a bothy (annexe). St Aidan's Roman Catholic Church has a 'camp' for needy youngsters staffed by volunteers of the Saint Vincent de Paul Society. Sister Tessa, of the Daughters of the Holy Cross, looks after the church. Marygate and Cambridge Houses provide simple accommodation and meals for educational, recreational and religious groups. The team who staff this form a temporary ecumenical community who daily meet for prayer. Two associates of the Northumbria Community, Mark and Mary Fleeson, run the scriptorium. Our own Community of Aidan and Hilda, along with several of these I have mentioned, try to be available to visitors who seek spiritual guidance, prayer, retreats and other resources. Together, we offer a weekly healing service.

The religious elements of this village have grown piecemeal out of the deeply earthed rhythmns of the natural village – fishing and farming. It has no shared Rule or set of values to hold it together. It requires incomers to honour the primary place of the small fishing and farming community, to 'live in humility, preferring one another' (Philippians 2:3). Providentially its nature space is safeguarded by *Natural England*, its shop and tourist space is guarded by the tide which encircles the island daily. This discourages those kinds of businesses that want to gain maximum profit for no personal care, since mainland outlets can remain open for longer.

I pointed out in chapter 1 that movements such as *Focolare* have little cities. Chapter 5 pointed to warehouse and larger churches that incorporate several features of a village of God, and there are towns in the UK where Churches Together espouse these features.

A proposal for a village of God around a cathedral

Cathedrals are the church's best assets. They are well attended, maintain daily prayer and often have a shop, restaurant and visual resources. I have found recent books on the role of the Church of England cathedrals disappointing. *Flagships of the Spirit: Cathedrals in Society*[83] focused on a cathedral's asset as a building, but a cathedral can be so much more than that; we need to explore its asset as a community.

Most cathedrals, in the British Isles at least, have a close in which live a few cathedral staff and a larger number of the general public who rent properties from the cathedral. Here is a simple plan of action by which a cathedral can become a transforming community at the heart of its city. The Dean and Chapter draw up a Rule of Life which sets out the vision, values and practices of daily prayer and mission which 'the Cathedral Community' lives by. They invite any existing worshippers and residents to adopt this. When a cathedral property becomes vacant it is offered, in the first place, to someone who adopts the Rule. Prayer, hospitality and outreach will be three key components of the Rule.

[83] Platten, Stephen & Lewis, Christopher (eds) (1998) *Flagships of the Spirit: Cathedrals in Society*, DLT.

The sublime choral evensongs will continue, but they will not be the only arrow in the cathedral's bow. Taizé-style services of vigil and chant, charismatic praise led by bands, and open-air worship to celebrate full moons will offer something for everyone. A refectory and a study centre are already typical signs of a cathedral's hospitality: emerging cathedrals might develop evening street cafés, hostel and bed and breakfast accommodation. Wedding couples, including those who can pay little, will be welcome to picnic in the cloisters. Prayer stations, spiritual advisors, a retreat house and internet link-up will be part of the scene. Those who follow the Rule will be offered spiritual formation and soul friends, and they themselves will offer this to people from the wider community.

Proposals for a village of God in London

By and large, the challenge to develop villages of God at the heart of our society still lies in the future. Lateral thinking and inspired leadership is needed. The time has come for Christian leaders to plan for a village of God in each capital city. This can begin with brainstorming. Even if it ends with less than was hoped for, little is better than nothing. In this spirit I 'speak like a fool (2 corinthians 11:17)' and make a proposal for London. It involves the three most unlikely bedfellows on London's Christian scene. Before you dismiss it, ponder these words of Ian Bradley in his book *You've Got to Have a Dream: The Message of the Musical*.[84]

> For Christians, for the Church, for all humanity, as for Lieutenant Cable, 'you gotta have a dream – if you don't have a dream, how you gonna have a dream come true?'

[84] Bradley, Ian (2004) *You've Got to Have a Dream: The Message of the Musical*, SCM Press.

I propose that Brompton Oratory, Holy Trinity Church Brompton, and the Russian Orthodox Cathedral make a covenant. They will offer their sites and resources to establish the vision and values of a village of God. This village will be a sign of unity in diversity, of the Trinity at the heart of London.

The Oratory's building is the second largest Roman Catholic Church in London. The Oratorian Fathers are a group of secular priests who live in community, bound together in charity, and who follow the Rule of Life of Saint Philip Neri (1515–1595). Their principal apostolate is the celebration of the Sacred Liturgy, preaching and hearing confessions. Over 3000 Londoners of all ages worship every Sunday in this enormous High Renaissance Early Baroque church. Its choir is renowned for preserving the Church's treasury of sacred music of Gregorian Chant and polyphony. Vespers and Benediction are celebrated in the traditional rite every Sunday afternoon, followed by a procession to the Lady Altar, where prayers are offered for the conversion of England. Six masses are offered on weekdays (one in Latin) and a Holy Hour is held on one evening during the week, with Benediction on another. The annual Forty Hours devotion, and the Corpus Christi procession out into Brompton Road ends with over 1000 people present at the Benediction. Confessions are heard daily. The monthly *Parish Magazine* lists over twenty organisations, including two excellent Catholic schools, one primary, one secondary; courses in the Catholic faith, Sacred Scripture, and spirituality; a library; a bookshop; a conference of the Society of Saint Vincent de Paul; groups of young people, and more. Parishioners are encouraged to join pilgrimages. The garden of the Oratory House, one of the largest inner London private gardens, hosts a variety of stalls and activities. Other fund-raising events include exhibitions, concerts and recitals by parishioners and other artists of high calibre. Oratorian Father Charles Dilke warned the congregation not to look inward at Solemn Mass.

On Home Mission Sunday 2008, he said:

> the Mass . . . is for the glory of Almighty God and to
> provide a basis from which those who participate can
> go out and engage in the labour of God's vineyard.

There is a high wall between The Oratory and Holy Trinity
Church next door. I propose that they envision both areas as
God's vineyard, put in gates and open these sites, the pilgrim-
ages and the events to members of the village.

Holy Trinity is one of the Church of England's most thriving
charismatic churches. It has planted or replanted many daughter
churches throughout London. It birthed the worldwide Alpha
courses which have brought new faith to millions. It is also a
charitable trust which employs staff for an impressive range of
enterprises. It is home to St Paul's Theological Centre, has
a bookshop and a venue in its grounds for conferences. In
addition to its sizeable grassed area, which also houses the
vicarage, it raises revenue by charging business people to park
their cars in its car park on weekdays. I am told there is now a
plan to create underground facilities.

I propose that they also build cells round the edge of the
grass area, and recruit young people to live in them and take
vows for two or more years. Market stalls will replace cars on
weekdays. These will be run by members from the three parts
of the village, and will include fair trade, third world, healing,
local craft and art, whole food, produce from prisoners and
asylum seekers, and up-market pilgrims' aids. A joint book and
resources shop will be built in this area which will be open
daily. There will also be an exhibition area, computer and café
facilities. Poustinias will be built on the quiet, Oratory side of
the wall which anyone may rent for a day's DIY retreat.

A pilgrim trail will lead from Holy Trinity grounds to the
Russian Orthodox Cathedral in Ennismore Gardens at the rear.

Planning permission will be sought for contemporary icons and scriptural plaques to grace the pathway. The cathedral and its bookshops will be open at all times because it will be complemented by volunteer staff from the village of God. The cathedral will sustain a school of Orthodox and desert spirituality and prayer which may use any of the three venues. The blessed bread which it offers to all at the end of each Liturgy will be brought in basketfuls to the other parts of the village, and there will be an Orthodox presence in the stalls. The village will have an arrangement with Harrods and other local stores to take prayer request slips left by shoppers to the Intercession Centre at the cathedral. Here, lay and ordained singers will offer these up and thousands of prayer candles will be lit in return for a donation. As concert-goers leave the nearby Royal Albert Hall they will see a phalanx of candles and signs leading to a coffee facility and prayer stations, and the trail to the rest of the village. The cathedral will be the venue for concerts of religious music sponsored by the village. Young Russian recruits will be housed in the Holy Trinity cells. Their vows will not be confused with canonical monastic regulations; they will have the blessing of the Bishop as an expression of their personal devotion to God.

This will require no change in canonical regulations. It will be a slow, gentle process. Those who have made the covenant and taken the two-year vows may in time subscribe to an ecumenical Rule. This requires each to be true to their own church, to relate transparently to other members of the village as brothers and sisters in Christ and to support certain common observances. These may include an annual procession of witness, retreat, and agape, a weekly healing service, and daily prayer. The village as a whole will provide life coaches, prayer guides, and daily meditation. A small council of one or two representatives of each church will serve the village.

Before this vision is dismissed, think about this:

The most well-attended monasteries in Britain are Buddhist. Young people, Christian, Buddhist or of no belief, are drawn to them by the experience of community, peace and beauty, not necessarily by the actual Buddhist beliefs which often do not satisfy. Kagyu Samyé Ling Monastery and Tibetan Centre Eskdalemuir is the largest Tibetan Buddhist centre in Western Europe. Anyone may visit, and may relate easily to it in a variety of ways. They can visit the centre for the day and spend time walking around the grounds, meditating in the temple, relaxing in the café and browsing in the shop. It is open all day long every day of the year. They may also stay overnight in the guest house and attend one of the courses or retreats, or just simply relax and enjoy the peaceful atmosphere.

They may work as a volunteer on a daily basis, coming and going each day, or they can stay there as a visitor or resident. Volunteering jobs include gardening, lighting lamps for world peace, chopping vegetables and cleaning. In order to become a resident you are required to stay at Samyé Ling for one month as a paying guest to see if this is the right place for you to live. If you would like to become a monk or nun you should already have taken refuge as a Buddhist and will be asked to observe lay vows for six months to see if you are happy with the monastic lifestyle. You will also need to discuss your plans with the abbot.

Another way of participating and supporting the work of Samyé Ling is to make donations to the ongoing projects such as the Samyé Monastery Project, which is currently in the third and final phase. When completed, Phase 3 will provide accommodation for students and nuns as well as housing a library, audio and other facilities.

Where will there be Christian monasteries that are as accessible as this? Where will be the monastically minded churches that fly large, beautiful prayer flags such as grace the Tibetan monasteries, letting the winds carry the prayers of the people to the four corners of the earth for all to see?

Conclusion

This book began with a survey of experiments that might loosely be described as 'new monasticism', and pointed to fresh thinking from the old monasticism. In chapter two I drew out certain human and flexible aspects of past monasticism that are often missed by those who see in monasticism only a single stereotype.

I then looked at the challenges to new monasticism. Is it really any different from the old monasticism? If it is, in what ways, and can it be sustained without, for example, celibacy or daily prayer? I then examined the idea that the essence of monastic life is what everyone is called to live – it is universal. I highlighted certain qualities of the 'universal monk' within each of us that we can aspire to and work to acquire.

The final chapter asked whether the multitude of small communities emerging in out-of-the-way places might signify a sea change in the world, but argued that if this is to offer the world a third way between greed-driven capitalism and hate-driven fundamentalism, the monastery needed to come into the high (main) street. How might this happen? Could churches become monasteries? (Not likely but not impossible.) Could monasteries become churches? (Difficult, but it has happened before, notably with the early Irish churches.) I cited an example of how an ordinary congregation could adopt a Rule, soul friends and a daily rhythm of prayer.

There can be no doubt that the social framework to which today's monastics have to relate differs from that of any previous period and that this brings new challenges. Without community, capitalism may implode. Capitalism, according to widely held belief, is the freedom for any business to make profits. A society whose chief god is 'the market', however, cannot survive. Creative capitalism, as promoted by people such as Bill Gates, founder of Microsoft, is an attempt to blend social awareness with the market. The aim of creative capitalism is to do good (often with a nudge from socially aware activists) and to make a profit at the same time. Even with creative capitalism, however, rich countries are likely to break down if the building block of community is absent. The people become climbers, by fair means or foul, the losers become addicts or knifers; families, institutions and communities fall apart. In his book *Fishing in Utopia*'[85] that astute social observer Andrew Brown recalls the Sweden of the 1970s as a widely envied social democratic paradise. Money was spent on health, education and welfare. When he returned recently he was horrified to find that social cohesion was wilting under the pressure of consumerism and globalisation. The reason Sweden's experiment worked at first, he concludes, is that its people were only a few generations away from living off the land, so the disciplines of frugality and solidarity were ingrained in them. Now, these disciplines are being lost – money alone cannot sustain community.

The massive changes required if planet earth is to survive in its present form, and if billions of lives are not to be lost in degradation and death, requires an equally massive leap of the imagination and bold new lateral thinking from church leaders. That is why I brainstormed (some would say, foolishly) an imaginary scenario of a coming together of three actual Anglican, Orthodox and Roman Catholic churches who are neighbours in the heart of London. These three particular churches may not make this vision become a reality, although if they had the will, they could. Others, however, catching the vision, may run with it, perhaps in the unlikeliest of places, although for others, in and out of struggling churches, this may seem inaccessible.

That is where villages of God come into their own. Whether they are on one site, a local federation of facilities, or virtual,

[85] Brown, Andrew (2008) *Fishing in Utopia: Sweden and the future that disappeared*, Granta Books.

whether they are in early or advanced stages of evolution, they hold out the hands of possibility. Each person, project and church can see themselves as a part of a greater whole, and work towards the achievement of modelling an alternative society.

Terrible winds from the four quarters of the world – economic, climatic, political and religious – threaten to tear us apart. Could the new monastic villages provide a heart for our global village which outlives them all?

Followers of the Way: Biblical Foundations for Monastic Living

By Simon Reed

Introduction

Ever since monasticism began to blossom as a strange flower in the Egyptian deserts of the third century, it has for the most part existed on the edges of Christian experience, often admired as a prophetic or protest movement, but also condemned as a form of religious elitism or spiritual self-indulgence. In Protestant Europe this latter view ultimately prevailed when the sixteenth-century Reformation dealt a life-threatening blow to many monastic institutions, albeit that they had departed far from their original ideals. This reinforced a separation from the Eastern roots of monasticism and their later expression in that part of the first millennium Christian world which can be described by the controversial shorthand of 'the Celtic church'.[86] By contrast, fourth-century Christian leaders like Athanasius, Basil the Great and John Chrysostom saw monasticism 'not as a special form of the Christian life but as the actualisation of what was in principle demanded of all Christians'.[87] Whilst Basil founded and organised monastic communities in the conventional sense, it is quite clear that writings like *The Longer Rules*[88] are intended for the guidance of all Christians. Monasticism was, to borrow a recent political phrase, for the

---

[86] There is a heated debate among scholars about what precisely is meant by the 'Celtic church' and even whether the expression should be used at all.

[87] Greer, Rowan A. (1986) *Broken Lights and Mended Lives: Theology and Common Life in the Early Church,* Pennsylvania University Press, 163.

[88] Saint Basil, trans. Sister M. Monica Wagner (1962) *Ascetical Works, The Fathers of the Church,* vol. 9, The Catholic University of America Press, 223–337.

many and not just for the few. Turning to Western Christianity, Ian Bradley has persuasively argued that 'for Christians living in the British Isles between the fifth and eleventh centuries, the monastery rather than the parish church was the primary focus for worship, pastoral care, and religious instruction.'[89] Here, it seems, monasticism was not just for the many. It was, in effect, for all.

Even as brief a historical survey as this highlights some fascinating questions. Would it be beneficial to revive the Eastern and Celtic model of monasticism as the normal Christian life, and would it be possible to do so? More fundamentally, is this a correct understanding of how the Christian life could, and indeed should, be lived? These are not simply pragmatic questions, but theological ones too. Our starting point, therefore, must be to ask what evidence the Bible gives to support a monastic understanding and model of the Christian life, and it is that question which this paper will set out to answer.

First, we must try to define monasticism in order to know what we are actually looking for in the Bible. One possible starting point would be the idea of community, but this will not get us very far. Both Old Testament and New Testament faith is irreducibly communal, whether expressed as the people of Israel or the body of Christ. Furthermore, the development of monasticism, even in its earliest days, has spawned a variety of different forms of common life. A more helpful starting place is Ian Bradley's observation that:

> monasteries are ... where people go willingly to live under rules and authority. They are communities of intention, made up of those who have taken certain vows and accepted a certain lifestyle.[90]

---

[89] Bradley, Ian (2000) *Colonies of Heaven: Celtic Models for Today's Church*, Darton, Longman & Todd.
[90] Bradley, Ian *Colonies of Heaven*, 8.

Monasticism may therefore be defined not merely as people who are seeking to live solely (*monos*) for God, but doing so with a communal accountability based upon a commitment to a shared rule or way of life. It is fascinating to observe that the earliest self-designation of the followers of Jesus Christ, before they were first called Christians (Acts 11:26), was 'the Way' (*ho hodos*, Acts 9:2), a name which is used no less than seven times throughout Acts.[91] For our purposes this is a curiously evocative term, made even more fascinating because of the scholarly uncertainty about where it originates or precisely what it means. Gerhard Ebel however points in a helpful direction when he summarises it as: 'a designation for Christians and their proclamation of Jesus Christ, which includes the fact that *this proclamation also comprises a particular walk of life or way.*'[92]

Monastic groups in the Bible?

Attempts have been made to find biblical prototypes for the kinds of communities defined by a way of life which appeared with the rise of what we now call monasticism. Examples have been found but their value to this investigation is limited. First there are the Nazirites, whose rules are set down in Numbers 6:1–21 and who are described by Gordon Wenham as 'the monks and nuns of ancient Israel'.[93] It is interesting that for all his championing of a law-free Gospel, Paul both takes and affirms Nazirite vows in Acts 18:18 and 21:23–26. Second, and similar to the Nazirites, there are the vows of the Rechabites (2 Kings 10:15 and 23; Jeremiah 35; 1 Chronicles 2:55) whom both J. A. Thompson and Gerhard von Rad see as standing up for the purity of Israel's ancient religion during times of

[91] Acts 9:2; 18:25-26; 19:9, 23; 24:14, 22.
[92] Ebel, Gerhard, *ho hodos*, in, Colin Brown (ed.) (1975–78) *The New International Dictionary of Christian Theology,* The Paternoster Press, III, 935–943.
[93] Wenham, Gordon J. (1981) *Numbers,* Inter-Varsity Press, 85.

syncretism and compromise.[94] Third, there are the 'companies of prophets' associated with Samuel (1 Samuel 19:18–24), Elijah and particularly Elisha (1 Kings 20:35; 2 Kings 2:3 *passim*). These are distinctive communities and von Rad even goes so far as to suggest that they 'lived according to rule' but he is unable to bring forward any evidence to support this latter claim.[95]

Examples from the New Testament are even thinner on the ground. John the Baptist certainly resembles a Nazirite (cf. Luke 1:15) but despite having a following of disciples he does not form any kind of distinctive community. The early church in Jerusalem followed the prayer patterns of the temple and shared property in common, possibly inspired by the Jewish Essene community which also had a presence in the city. However there is no evidence that this practice was taken on anywhere else, or that it survived the scattering of the church after the martyrdom of Stephen. Lastly there is the enrollment of widows described in 1 Timothy 5:3–16, but it is more likely that this teaching is trying to regulate care for those in genuine need, rather than describing some kind of proto-religious order.

What this summary demonstrates is that whilst a narrow base of evidence can be found in the Bible to support the existence of distinct communities living by some kind of rule of life, none of them embrace the mainstream of either Jewish or Christian religious life, and with their frequent links to either prophecy or protest, provide at best a foundation for a minority monasticism of the margins which is far removed from the vision of Basil or the practice of the Celtic Church.

---

[94] Thompson, J. A. (1980) *Jeremiah*, Eerdmans, 618–619; Von Rad, Gerhard (1975) *Old Testament Theology*, vol. 1, SCM Press, 63–64.

[95] Von Rad, Gerhard (1975) *Old Testament Theology*, vol. 2, SCM Press, 26.

Ways of life in the Old Testament

Turning away from minority groups to the mainstream of biblical religion, we see immediately that Old Testament faith was expressed through community and covenant. To be one of God's elect nation was not merely a matter of birth, but also of being faithful to the terms of God's covenant promise as set down in the Torah, the Law of Moses. To be an Israelite was by definition to be a member of a distinctive community which lived by a rule of life. The five books of Moses, however, are an enormous body of material to master, whatever view one takes of their process of composition. What is fascinating for our purposes is that within the larger body of Old Testament legal material, and later in the prophets, are shorter sections which, in von Rad's words, 'endeavour to outline Jahweh's whole will for men in the shortest possible form'.[96]

The most famous example of this is of course the Ten Commandments (Exodus 20:2–17 and Deuteronomy 5:6–21). These are explicitly prefaced by the explanation that they are the guidelines for how to live as 'a priestly kingdom and a holy nation' (Exodus 19:5–6). What is less widely recognised is that although these by their setting have pride of place, there are other equally ancient outlines of the lifestyle God seeks from his people embedded within the books of the Torah.

Old Testament legal language uses a number of recognisable forms and Exodus 21:12, 15–17 and 22:19–20 contain six statements all beginning with the word 'whoever'. These are thought to be derived from another ancient summary of the law which embraces purity in worship, respect for parents, and non-exploitation of others. Leviticus 19:11 and 13–18 provides another such summary using the familiar 'you shall not' form of commandment. This longer summary again highlights purity in worship, along with good relationships within the community

[96] Von Rad, *Theology*, vol. 1, 191.

and a robust concern for just treatment of the vulnerable. The third example is the twelve curses of Deuteronomy 27:12–26, the so-called Dodecalogue of Shechem. Just like the Ten Commandments, this material is placed in a highly significant position, presented as Moses' parting speech before the people enter the Promised Land. The dramatic setting and simple structure make the material easily memorable, and suggest that it was intended to be used as such, a simple guideline to help the Israelites from going astray once they were in the land. The contents are by now familiar: fidelity to God, upholding of the family, justice within the nation, and compassion for the poor. References to boundary markers (verse 17) and roads (verse 18) support the view that this particular way of life is for settlers rather than nomads.

This tendency to produce tailored summaries of how covenant faithfulness is to be expressed is not unique to the books of Moses. Psalm 15:1–5 is an ethical check-list for a pilgrim arriving at Jerusalem for one of the major festivals. Fidelity to Israel's God is taken for granted under such circumstances and so the focus is on behaviour towards others with a concern for truthfulness of speech, keeping of oaths, avoidance of bribes and usury, positive behaviour towards fellow God-fearing Israelites, and separation from evil-doers. This way of life therefore promotes harmony and just living to build up the community of Israel. Similar values are to be found, expressed succinctly and in broad brush terms, in the definition of 'the fear of the Lord' to be found in Psalm 34:11–18. Three elements feature here, highlighting truthfulness of speech, the embracing of good and separation from evil.

Surprisingly perhaps, the book of Proverbs has little to offer in this discussion. In one sense the entire book contributes towards a life shaped by God-fearing wisdom, however what it lacks are the kinds of distinctive and memorable summaries which can be identified as offering a simple and easily memorable way of life. The closest approach to this is the seven things the Lord hates and abominates in Proverbs 6:16–19, embracing the now-familiar elements of truthfulness of speech, fidelity to family, and upholding of justice.

Turning to the prophetic literature, a great deal of it deals, unsurprisingly, with a denunciation of Israel's infidelity and injustice, and failure to live in the fear of the Lord. Micah 6:8 offers a three-element summary of what God requires, embracing just behaviour, generosity to others and faithfulness to him. However, the passage suffers from difficulties of precise translation, and it is embedded in a larger context of reproach for Israel's failures in these and others areas. Vastly more significant material is to be found in the book of Ezekiel, set as it is in the early stages of the exile but already looking beyond to the reconstruction and definition of Israel beyond this cataclysmic disaster. The material, stated positively in Ezekiel 18:5–9 and negatively in Ezekiel 18:14–17, is worth citing in full, with its structure highlighted:

- If a man is righteous and does what is lawful and right,

- if he does not eat upon the mountains [or eat the blood] or lift up his eyes to the idols of the house of Israel

- does not defile his neighbour's wife (or approach a woman during her menstrual period, *omitted in verses 14–17*)

- does not oppress anyone,

- but restores to the debtor his pledge,

- commits no robbery,

- gives his bread to the hungry and covers the naked with a garment,

- does not take advance or accrued interest,

- withholds his hand from iniquity,

- (executes true justice between contending parties, *omitted in verses 14–17*)

- follows my statutes, and is careful to observe my ordinances, acting faithfully,

- such a one is righteous; he shall surely live, says the Lord God.

In his commentary on Ezekiel, Walther Eichrodt argues that this comprises a new summary of the law for a new situation, a selection suitable for exiles, 'a norm for moral and social life, which can provide a firm basis for a man's relations with his neighbour in a foreign land'.[97]

Once again we see the now familiar elements of true worship of God, protection of family, and the obligations of social justice. Eichrodt prefers the translation which forbids eating blood rather than eating at the mountain shrines of other gods since this would be more relevant in the setting of the exile in Babylon. Again this way of life is characterised by accessible simplicity and immediate contextual relevance. Ezekiel 22:6–12 expresses negatively a corresponding way of life for the inhabitants of Jerusalem. Appropriately this has a stronger emphasis on faithfulness in worship and religious observance, and also emphasises just treatment of foreigners. Commenting on the way of life for exiles, Eichrodt makes helpful remarks on how any biblical way of life must be understood: 'A man may fulfil all the above-mentioned commands, and as a result be termed righteous. This . . . does not mean that he is sinless . . . but that he is a willing member of the . . . community . . . and shows a right attitude towards the covenant relationship.'[98]

---

[97] Eichrodt, Walther (1970) *Ezekiel*, SCM Press, 239.
[98] Eichrodt, ibid. 239–240.

We therefore take our leave of the Old Testament with a passage which corresponds exactly to the definition of monasticism with which we set out to explore: people who are seeking to live solely for God, but doing so with a communal accountability based upon a commitment to a shared rule or way of life.

Ways of life in the New Testament

If the ways of life we find in the Old Testament are abbreviations of Torah, given as simple guidelines for righteous living and adapted to particular cultural or geographical settings, we confront a serious historical and theological problem in the New Testament, namely the view of the Law expressed in the Gospels and the epistles. The historical context of Jesus' ministry is in a community living with a legacy of failure to be faithful to their covenant obligations. Israel has returned from exile in Babylon centuries previously, but the former glories have not returned with them and the promised blessings have not been fulfilled. The Sadducees in the temple attempt to maintain religious and social business as usual, albeit under Roman oversight, the Essenes withdraw to create a sectarian alternative in the desert at Qumran, the Pharisees advocate radical observance of the law as the way to restore divine blessing, whilst others, later called Zealots, begin to turn directly to armed resistance. Into all of this comes Jesus, proclaiming that the kingdom of God is now at hand, demonstrating the nature of this kingdom by works of healing, deliverance, and the inclusion of outcasts, and explaining it by challenging and subversive stories. He also teaches a new way of life which for Matthew, and the subsequent centuries of Christianity, is summed up in the Sermon on the Mount.

Jesus and the Sermon on the Mount

If simplicity is the common feature of the ways of life we have examined so far, the jungle of scholarly literature generated by these three chapters would suggest that the popular claim to 'live by the Sermon on the Mount' is anything but simple. There are real issues here. From a historical perspective Jesus' own attitude to the Law caused much controversy in his own time, and subsequently Paul radically revises the entire place of the Law within Christian life. Where then does the Sermon on the Mount belong? From an ethical perspective, the Sermon has often been treated as timeless truths without a historical context, generating endless disputes about interpretation and application. It is impossible within the scope of this study to engage with even a fraction of the larger scholarly debate. However, N. T. Wright's comprehensive and expanding historical work, particularly in *Jesus and the Victory of God*, offers a particularly helpful perspective on the Sermon for our purposes.[99]

Wright begins by noting that the Old Testament context for righteous living is the covenant. Jesus' core message concerns the kingdom of God which, understood in its Jewish Old Testament context, means the renewal of that covenant. In the prophetic literature, intertwined with promises of covenant renewal are promises that in this renewal, the covenant people will receive from God a new heart which will enable them to keep the covenant. This hope is first articulated in Deuteronomy 30:6–10: 'the Lord your God will circumcise your heart ... so that you will love the Lord your God with all your heart and with all your soul, in order that you may live. Then you shall again obey the Lord, observing all his commandments ...' It is proclaimed in Jeremiah 31:31–34 with its promise of the law written on the hearts of the new covenant people, and supremely

[99] Wright, N. T. (1996) *Jesus and the Victory of God*, SPCK, 274–297.

in Ezekiel 36:24–27: 'a new heart I will give you, and a new spirit I will put within you…and make you follow my statutes and be careful to observe my ordinances.' By contrast, Jesus is frequently critical of the hardness of heart which keeps people from understanding and embracing the way of the kingdom (e.g. Mark 3:5; 6:52; 7:6–8; 7:20–23; 8:17). The kingdom however meant the renewing of the covenant and by implication the renewing of the hearts of the people, and hence it was entirely appropriate that 'Jesus' retelling of Israel's story included the call and challenge … to live as the renewed Israel, the people of the new covenant'.[100] The Sermon on the Mount offers a simply expressed and context-sensitive way of life for this renewed people, whether viewed as a single discourse or a gathered compendium of teaching, and considering the similar material in Luke 6:20–49, it is entirely plausible that Jesus would have done both.[101]

We are often so used to pondering single sayings or well-known sections of the Sermon that we do not have a sense of its overall shape and structure. The following outline is based on Wright's discussion on Matthew 5:1–7:29:

5:3–12	Beatitudes – heart qualities of those seeking the kingdom
5:13–16	Call to be the true Israel in the world
5:17–20	True fulfilment of the law
5:21–48	How to live the heart of the law • murder and anger • adultery and divorce • oaths and truthfulness • vengeance • hatred of enemies

[100] Wright, ibid. 275.
[101] Wright, ibid. 287.

6:1–34	How to worship God from the heart
	• alms-giving
	• prayer
	• fasting
	• wealth and possessions
7:1–6	Avoid condemning
7:7–11	Ask and receive
7:12	The Golden Rule
7:13–23	Beware counterfeits
7:24–27	Be the true temple ('house') which stands firm

Presented like this, the Sermon spells out in practical terms the values of generosity and jubilee embodied in the parables and prophetic actions of Jesus. It also treads a clear and careful path between the alternative ways of life presented as routes to the kingdom by Jesus' contemporaries, the violent resistance of the insurrectionists and the radical law observance of the Pharisees. Whilst observing that the Sermon can 'be generalised into a universal ethic,' Wright is emphatic that it 'makes excellent sense in a Palestinian setting in the first third of the first century . . . It addresses directly the question people were asking: how to be faithful to YHWH (Yahweh/God) in a time of great stress and ambiguity . . . It offers a set of specific kingdom-agendas consonant with the rest of Jesus' specific message.'[102] In short, what we have here is Jesus' own simple, memorable, context-sensitive way of life for kingdom people.

---

[102] Wright, ibid., 292.

Paul and Gentile Christianity

The biggest test for the Jesus-centred movement was how it would adapt once it moved beyond the Jewish world where it came into being. The Jerusalem conference in Acts 15 depicts the resolution of the issue over whether Gentiles had to take on Jewish legal observances in order to become Christians. The guidelines in the resulting pastoral letter should be seen more as the details of an interim ruling designed to avoid causing undue offence to Jews than elements of a way of life for Gentile Christians. To see how Christianity was to be lived in the Gentile world we must turn to the body of letters attributed to Paul.

At first sight it might seem a fruitless task to find material in Paul which corresponds to our findings so far. He is, after all, adamant that 'we are discharged from the law, dead to that which held us captive, so that we are slaves not under the old written code but in the new life of the Spirit' (Romans 7:6). He asks the Colossians, 'Why do you submit to regulations? All these... are simply human commands and teachings. These have indeed an appearance of wisdom in promoting self-imposed piety, humility, and severe treatment of the body, but they are of no value in checking self-indulgence' (Colossians 2:21–23). Nevertheless he rejoices in telling the Romans that they 'have become obedient from the heart to the form of teaching to which [they] were entrusted, and that . . . having been set free from sin, [they] have become slaves of righteousness' (Romans 6:17–18), and does not hesitate to describe what this righteousness looks like in practice. As we shall see, the 'ethical' material which makes up the final section of many of Paul's letters is not simply specific advice to particular congregations or practical application of the preceding 'theological sections,' but a simple way of life for Spirit-filled believers in Christ, often addressing specific issues relevant to their cultural or geographical setting.

The chronology of Paul's letters is still debated, with

Galatians and 1 Thessalonians being the two contenders for the earliest letter. Without pre-judging that debate, we shall consider Galatians first because it demonstrates most clearly how Paul's understanding of what God has done in Christ issues in a clearly defined way of life. Galatians addresses a very specific problem, the dominance in that church of the view that Christians must take on observance of the Jewish law in order to be truly the people of God. This in turn was causing distress and discord amongst the mixed Jewish-Gentile congregation. Having explained justification by faith and the purpose of the Law, he expressed in no uncertain terms his opinion of those who insist Gentile converts should be circumcised, and reaffirmed the freedom which comes through faith in Christ. Paul concludes by setting out what this freedom means. 'You were called to freedom, brothers and sisters,' Paul writes, 'only do not use your freedom as an opportunity for self-indulgence, but through love become slaves to one another. For the whole law is summed up in a single commandment, "You shall love your neighbour as yourself" (Galatians 5:13–14). This is briefly contrasted with the back-biting disputes in Galatia (v.15). Christian freedom, then, is above all the freedom to love others because in Christ and through the Spirit we now have the ability to do so. For Paul it is the Spirit who shapes and empowers the Christian life and so he goes on to make his famous descriptive contrast of the works of the flesh and the fruit of the Spirit (vv.16–25). It is vital to emphasise that the fruit of the Spirit are just that: the fruit the Spirit produces, not something the believer causes to happen. Nevertheless, and in the light of all this, Paul does go on to spell out very specifically what actions are consonant with this Spirit-empowered law of love:

- Let us not become conceited, competing against one another, envying one another (5:26)

- If anyone is detected in a transgression . . . restore such a one in a spirit of gentleness (6:1)

- Bear one another's burdens, and in this way . . . fulfil the law of Christ (6:2)

- Those who are taught the word must share in all good things with their teacher (6:6)

Paul is clear that the primary fruit of the Spirit is love but wants his readers to recognise what love looks like in day-to-day life. In continuity with the practice of the Old Testament and the teaching of Jesus he is arguably setting out a simple way of life which is tailored to the needs of relatively new Christians, and therefore needs to be simple, and which also addresses the specific context of the issues raised by the disputes in Galatia.

1 Thessalonians sees Paul addressing a different situation. According to Acts 17:1–10, Paul and Silas were only able to spend the briefest period of time in the city after having planted the church there before being forcibly evicted by Jewish opponents. The letter is the first contact after these events with the fledgling congregation which despite its core of Jewish converts also contains a great many Gentile converts desperately in need of further Christian teaching. As in Galatians, Paul spells out the way of life of those who are believers in Christ, this time sandwiching it around a longer passage giving necessary teaching on the resurrection and the coming of the Lord:

> We ask and urge you in the Lord Jesus that, as you learned from us how you ought to live in order to please God . . . you should do so more and more. For you know what instructions we gave you through the Lord Jesus (4:1–2).

- abstain from fornication (4:3–8)

- love the brothers and sisters (4:9–10)

- live quietly, mind your own affairs, work with your hands, be dependent on no one (4:11–12)

- respect those who . . . have charge of you in the Lord . . . (5:12)

- be at peace among yourselves (5:13)

- admonish the idlers, encourage the fainthearted, help the weak, be patient with all of them (5:14)

- see that none of you repays evil for evil, but always seek to do good to one another and to all (5:15)

- rejoice always, pray without ceasing, give thanks in all circumstances (5:16–18)

- do not quench the Spirit, do not despise the words of prophets, but test everything; hold fast to what is good; abstain from every form of evil (5:19–22)

The same elements of love for one another and corresponding respect for church leaders are present, augmented in this case with elements dealing with sexual purity, relationships with those outside the church, and discerning openness to the work of the Spirit. These latter elements would be particularly appropriate for Gentile converts lacking a Jewish ethical framework, living and working outside of one, and doubtless bringing a background of different spiritual experiences from their pagan religious origins. Paul has given them a succinct way of life, relevant to their context, dealing with relationships with God, one another, and the wider world.

The two letters to the Corinthians are of a different nature, responding to specific needs, questions, problems and issues, and contain no sections of teaching of the kind examined in Galatians and 1 Thessalonians. For the next example of this we need to turn to Romans which again demonstrates the way in which Paul's theology leads logically into a way of life. The doxology which concludes the exposition of the righteousness of God in the first eleven chapters of the letter is immediately followed by an exposition of what 'the obedience of faith' (Romans 1:5) looks like. 'I appeal to you therefore, brothers and sisters,' Paul writes, 'by the mercies of God, to present your bodies as a living sacrifice, holy and acceptable to God, which is your spiritual [or reasonable, logical, *logikos*] worship. Do not be conformed to this world, but be transformed by the renewing of your minds, so that you may discern what is the will of God – what is good and acceptable and perfect' (Romans 12:1–2). Although they are 'led by the Spirit' (8:14) and under 'the law of the Spirit' (8:2) rather than 'the old written code' which brought death (7:5–6), Paul still believes that it is necessary to explain where the Spirit will lead them and for them to understand what walking according to the Spirit looks like. What follows is a way of life with key elements which are very similar to those in Galatians and 1 Thessalonians, but with added elements which apply very appropriately to the Roman situation:

- think with sober judgement about your gifts (12:3–8)

- let love be genuine; hate what is evil, hold fast to what is good (12:9)

- love one another with mutual affection; outdo one another in showing honour (12:10)

- do not lag in zeal, be ardent in spirit, serve the Lord (12:11)

- rejoice in hope, be patient in suffering, persevere in prayer (12:12)

- contribute to the needs of the saints (12:13a)

- extend hospitality to strangers (12:13b)

- bless those who persecute you; bless and do not curse them (12:14)

- rejoice with those who rejoice, weep with those who weep. Live in harmony with one another; do not be haughty, but associate with the lowly, do not claim to be wiser than you are (12:15–16)

- do not repay anyone evil for evil, but take thought for what is noble in the sight of all. If it is possible ... live peaceably with all. Never avenge yourselves. 'If your enemies are hungry, feed them ...' Do not be overcome by evil, but overcome evil with good (12:17–21)

- be subject to the governing authorities (13:1–7)

- owe no one anything, except to love one another; for the one who loves another has fulfilled the law (13:8-10)

- welcome those who are weak in faith ... no longer pass judgement on one another ... never put a stumbling block in the way of another (14:1–15:13)

Distinctive to Romans is the teaching on submission to governing authorities which is of course immediately relevant in the capital of the empire but made even more so by the context of the recent expulsion of Jews from the city as troublemakers. The section also includes further detailed teaching dealing with the whole issue of dietary matters. Paul allows himself room to develop this in a letter which is not being written out of the need to address a particular problem but rather to introduce himself and his mission to a church which he did not personally plant. Nevertheless it is pressingly relevant given the mixed-race nature of the Roman church, a possible risk of Gentile Christians gloating over Jewish misfortunes, and central to Paul's vocation, so fully explained in the letter, to plant mixed-race churches. The Roman Christians would be left in no doubt about what Paul thought about God and the world, nor about the way of life he expected Christians to live out.

The last two letters with sections corresponding to those we have examined are Ephesians and Colossians. The Pauline authorship of these two letters has long been debated in mainstream scholarship but both Peter O'Brien and N. T. Wright have argued the Pauline authorship of the latter, and in a recent commentary on Ephesians John Muddiman has argued that large sections derive from Paul.[103] Whatever argument ultimately prevails, both letters are part of the Christian New Testament and highly relevant to our interests.

Ephesians is the most perfectly balanced epistle in the wider writings of St Paul with three chapters of theological exposition followed by a section of equal length drawing out its implications. Colossians is similarly well balanced. The latter epistle is explicitly intended for wider circulation (Colossians 4:16), and many scholars believe the same is true of Ephesians. If they are genuinely Pauline then they express his most mature and developed thoughts on what a Christian way of life should look like. Both letters are explicit that a Christian way of life is the logical outworking of a Christian self-understanding and identity. The section in Ephesians begins with an appeal to 'lead a life worthy of the calling to which you have been called, with all humility and gentleness, with patience, bearing with one another in love, making every effort to maintain the unity of the Spirit in the bond of peace . . . (4:1–3[16])' and therefore

[103] O'Brien, Peter T. (1982) *Colossians, Philemon*, Word Biblical Commentaries 44, Waco TX: Word Inc; Wright, N. T. (1986) *Colossians and Philemon*, Inter Varsity Press; Muddiman, John (2001) *The Epistle to the Ephesians*, Continuum.

to 'no longer live as the Gentiles live' (4:17f). The corresponding section in Colossians uses a similarly theological grounding: 'If you have been raised with Christ, set your minds on things that are above, not on things that are on earth, for you have died, and your life is hidden with Christ in God' (3:1–4). Both then go on to specify in detail what this will look like.

According to Ephesians this means:

- putting away falsehood, let all of us speak the truth to our neighbours, for we are members of one another (4:25)

- be angry but do not sin; do not let the sun go down on your anger, and do not make room for the devil (4:26–27)

- thieves must give up stealing; rather let them labour and work honestly with their own hands, so as to have something to share with the needy (4:28)

- let no evil talk come out of your mouths, but only what is useful for building up, as there is need, so that your words may give grace to those who hear. And do not grieve the Holy Spirit of God . . . (4:29–30)

- put away from you all bitterness and wrath and anger and wrangling and slander, together with all malice, and be kind to one another, tenderhearted, forgiving one another, as God in Christ has forgiven you (4:31–5:2)

- entirely out of place is obscene, silly, and vulgar talk; but instead, let there be thanksgiving (5:3–5)

- do not be associated with the disobedient. Try to find out what is pleasing to the Lord (5:6–14)

- do not get drunk with wine, be filled with the Spirit, singing to the Lord, giving thanks to God (5:15–20)

- be subject to one another out of reverence for Christ (5:21)

- wives be subject to your husbands as you are to the Lord (5:22–24)

- husbands, love your wives just as Christ loved the church (5:25–33)

- children, obey your parents in the Lord (6:1–3)

- fathers, do not provoke your children to anger (6:4)

- slaves, obey your earthly masters as you obey Christ (6:5–8)

- masters, stop threatening them (6:9)

- put on the whole armour of God (6:10–17)

- pray in the Spirit at all times (6:18–20).

According to Colossians it is to:

- put to death whatever in you is earthly: fornication, impurity, passion, evil desire, and greed (which is idolatry), anger, wrath, malice, slander, and abusive language from your mouth. Do not lie to one another (3:5–11)

- clothe yourselves with compassion, kindness, humility, meekness, and patience. Bear with one another and, if anyone has a complaint against another, forgive each other; just as the Lord has forgiven you, so you also must forgive. (3:12–15)

- let the word of Christ dwell in you richly; teach and admonish one another in all wisdom (3:16)

- with gratitude in your hearts sing psalms, hymns, and spiritual songs to God (3:16–17)

- wives, be subject to your husbands, as is fitting in the Lord (3:18)

- husbands, love your wives and never treat them harshly (3:19)

- children, obey your parents, for this is your acceptable duty in the Lord (3:20)

- fathers, do not provoke your children (3:21)

- slaves, obey your earthly masters wholeheartedly, fearing the Lord (3:22–25)

- masters, treat your slaves justly and fairly (4:1)

- devote yourselves to prayer, keeping alert in it with thanksgiving (4:2–4)

- Conduct yourselves wisely toward outsiders (4:5–6)

The similarities are obvious and the relationship between the two letters has been widely explored. The Ephesian emphasis on conflict with the forces of evil, the work of the Spirit, and prayer, has been persuasively shown by Clinton Arnold to be a response to the prominence of Ephesus as the home of the temple of Diana and a centre for the practice of magic.[104] Thus again we see the common features of the Pauline way of life being adapted to the local context. Within our larger discussion we see in Paul's fullest exposition of the Christian way of life the familiar elements we have found elsewhere in the Bible of relationship with God, love and generosity to others, the importance of family, and attention to just dealings and good relationships in the wider world.

[104] Arnold, Clinton E. (1989) *Ephesians: Power and Magic*, SNTS MS 63, Cambridge University Press.

Conclusion

We began by defining monasticism as people who are seeking to live solely for God, but doing so with a communal account-ability based upon a commitment to a shared rule or way of life. We noted the vision of the Eastern fathers of the church which saw monasticism not as a special form of the Christian life but as the actualisation of what was in principle demanded of all Christians. We saw this vision fulfilled in the Celtic mission which shaped Christianity in the British Isles so profoundly in the second half of the first millennium. Many contemporary Christians, such as the Community of Aidan and Hilda, are seeking a renewed church which recaptures in the third millennium the energy and impact of the first millennium church, and deliberately draw inspiration from the Celtic saints. This paper set out to answer the theological question of whether this 'new monasticism' reflects a correct understanding of how the Christian life could and should be lived by asking what evidence the Bible gives to support a monastic under-standing and model of the Christian life. In the Old Testament we found that in both the Law and the prophets are short, memorable, and context-sensitive summaries of how to live as the covenant people of God. We found that in the Sermon on the Mount Jesus set out a new way of life so that his contem-poraries could live as the people of the new covenant. Finally we found that Paul's letters contain similar context-sensitive material setting out the way of life of those who are led by the new law of the Spirit.

For Christians the Bible is both foundational and inspira-tional. We have established that the monastic practice of forming communities of believers, united by a shared commitment to a common way of life which attempts to express what a life lived wholly for God means in their time and context, is merely doing what the people of God throughout the Old and New

Testaments have always done. The first Christians were called followers of the Way. The new monasticism is rediscovering that way, and we should walk in it.